Poems
from the
Heron Clan VIII

Editors:

Adebimpe Oluwafunmilayo Adeyemi

Lillie Harward Delott

Nadine Hayes

Mary Jaimes-Serrano

Doug Stuber

Katherine James Books

Chapel Hill

katherinejamesbooks@gmail.com

Copyright 2021 Katherine James Books

All Rights revert to the poets.

ISBN: 978-1-7339299-3-6

Acknowledgements

"When I Walk Upon the Earth" was first published in the poetry collection: *When I Walk Upon the Earth* by **Jacqueline Belle,** Nov 28, 2019."Censored" was first published under the pen name, Moomii, by: Headline Poetry: #PoetofTheRevolution, 21 Nov 2019 https://lineriderpress.com/headlinepoetry/2019/09/21/censored/.

Trish Bennett: "Innisfree Me Arse!" This poem was Shortlisted in the Aurvivo / North West Words, Poetry Competition 2018, and published in North West Words Magazine, Issue 11, June 2019, and The Bangor Literary Journal, Issue 13, Dec 2020.

Nancy Corson Carter: " A Healing of Memory" is from *Dragon Poems Lewiston, NY: The Edwin Mellen Press, 1993).*

Robert Cumming: "Storm Light": earlier version in *Southern Poetry Review* and *Twenty: South Carolina Poetry Fellows.*

Bill Cushing: "Two Stairways," *Altadena Poetry Review* (2018), and in "*A Former Life.*"

Ginger Dehlinger: "Ghost Trees at Midnight" first appeared in the October 2019 edition of *Nightingale & Sparrow*, a literary magazine and small press.

Kitty Donnelly: "The Relative Who Lept" is from her book *The Impact of Limited Time,* Indigo Dreams Publishing, 2020.

Emmanuel Evans: "Broken" was first published at https://eoegroup.blogspot.com/2020/01/broken.html.

Attracta Fahy: "If I tell the Truth," was published in *The Comorant* July '19; "Despondency," was published in Banshee April '18; "Togher, Tuam Co. Galway: September 1987" was published in The Irish Times; October 2019 winner in New Irish Writing.

Kari Flickinger: "I Wandered Into A Beehive, and "branches, roots" were first published in *The Art of Self-Proclaimed Solitude,* 2019.

Jonathan Giles: An earlier version of "Resurrection" was published in *Better than Starbucks*, May 2019, Vol. IV, no 3.

Catherine Graham "The Buried" from *Winterkill* (Insomniac Press, 2010).

Sinead Griffin: "The Cormorant Comes After A Death" Fish Poetry Prize shortlist 2020

Kari Gunter-Seymour : "When You Meet My Mama," *Anthology of Appalachian Writers,* Volume XII; 'Last Night The Chime Of Tree Frogs," *A Place So Deep Inside America It Can't Be Seen* (Sheila-Na-Gig Editions 2020)*;* 'I Spoke To You Of Stars Instead," *A Place So Deep Inside America It Can't Be Seen* (Sheila-Na-Gig Editions 2020).

Lola Haskins: "Constellated," and "The Night After The Total Eclipse" first appeared in the *American Journal of Poetry;* "Mortality" appeared in Rattle. All three poems also appear in *Asylum Improvisations on John Clare,* 2019, University of Pittsburgh Press.

Wendy Holborow: "After the Silent Phone Call" first published by *Poetry Salzburg,* was featured on Poetry Kit's Caught in the Net, and was a finalist in The Atlanta Review competition 2016. Most recently it has been included in my latest collection *Shipwrecked,* 2020. "Shipwrecked Sun" is also included in the collection *Shipwrecked.*

Earl Carlton Huband: "Graduate School Experiment in Group Living" – *Pinesong Awards* (NC Poetry Society, 2019). "Love the Crooked Thing" – *The Road Not Taken* (http://journalformalpoetry.com, 2019).

Olaitan Humble: "Pa's Dream (Amaranthine)" was published in *All Guts No Glory Magazine* "Rhapsody" is published in *The African Writers Review.*

Linda Imbler: "Overlooking The Cliff" was previously published in *Literary Garland.*

Jerry Judge "Luna Moth," first appeared in *No Forwarding Address* by Jerry Judge, Palanquin Press of the University of South Carolina Aiken).

Tim Mattimoe: "Elegy In A Minor Key" appeared in *Bottle Boogie* (2016).

Deborah Melone: "Bonnarding" is from *Farmers' Market*, Every Other Thursday Press, copyright 2014.

Toti O'Brien: "Joan of Arc" was first published in *Gyroscope*, Spring 2019.

Carolyn Robinson: "All the Names" was first published in the book *I Write to Keep Me Sane.* Released August 2020.

Louise Runyon: "medlock school powwow 1988" appeared in my third book of poetry, *The Clearing* (2011).

Sanjeev Sethi: "Druthers" was first published in *The Stray Branch,* 2017.

Paul Sherman: "The Tire," was published in *Smoky Mountain River Adventures,* (Old Mountain Press, 2020).

Cindy B. Stevens: "Maybe I'm Dead" in *Naked,* (Main Street Rag Publishing Company), 2018.

Doug Stuber: "Rural Myth," first appeared in *Beatnik Cowboy,* 2020.

Priscilla Webster-Williams: "At Timberlake Earth Sanctuary" first appeared in *Chrysalis,* Vol.15, Fall 2018: a publication of The Center for Education, Imagination and the Natural World. Greensboro, NC

Jocelyn Wright: "Lost Beautiful Lives" appeared in: *Nonkilling Arts Research Committee Letter,* Vol. 4(6), November-December 2020, https://nonkilling.org/center/?mailpoet_router&endpoint=view_in_browser&action=view&data=WzgsIjM2NjBkNzFkYzQ0OCIsMCwwLDAsMV0

Introduction

Poems from the Heron Clan hatched in Rochester, NY in 1996. Doug Stuber, Ed Lyons and Richard Smyth, Ph.D., a librarian in Boston, were the core poets at inception. There were 19 poets in our first anthology, notably, Xue Di, a professor at Brown University who was rescued by the Freedom to Write program at Brown, from a dangerous jail in Beijing after the Tiananmen Square Massacre, where he stood with the protestors. We also published Ilya Kaminsky in an early publication for the current-day star.

It was six years between the first and second volume, and then another seven years before the third one was published. Since 2015, when Stuber returned from a seven-year professorship in S. Korea, the Heron Clan has been published annually, usually in April. Currently Smyth publishes and edits Albatross, which features eco-centric, tightly wound poetics. His poems in the Heron Clan have stretched past the boundaries of Albatross. Lyons has recently published Wachovia, detailing the history of the Moravian Church in Salem, NC in lyrical form.

About half the poets in later editions have resided in North Carolina; but in recent years, we have reached across the country. Australia, Brazil, Italy, South Korea, Thailand, India, Germany, Wales, England, Ireland, China and Russia have all been represented as well. Writers working at all levels are invited to submit. We aim to represent poets of color, well-established poets and emerging writers, young and mature poets. While our editorial board changes somewhat from year to year, we include men and women, and poets with expertise in different genres. We currently have four women, one man, one Nigerian, one African American and one Latinx editor. We don't have themes, other than diversity.

Thanks for reading.

To submit, send three poems and a 50-word bio to katherinejamesbooks@gmail.com

Table of Contents

Dedicated to J. Delaney Watson

We've known so many fine poets.

His poems will be the last we remember.

Lola Haskins

The Night after the Total Eclipse

we wanted to see stars so we drove past the villages with their closed pubs, past the odd house, past the darkened farms, past the walled monks' road, past Grassington, and after miles of dips and rises we turned into a field. But the moon was so huge, so swollen -- like lips after too much kissing-- that it paled the sky, and, looking up, we could not be sure of anything and should we have been adrift at sea, no sextant ever made could have saved us.

Lola Haskins

Serenade

Soon your small yellow leaves
will become meteors

falling through the dark as
each of us will fall

no matter how hard we love,
no matter how close we come

to composing a line the angels
would recite, if only there

were such a perfect line,
if only there were angels.

Lola Haskins

Constellated

When the atoms in my body

return to stars

They will not remember

this five am

out my window,

neither the moor

asleep on the horizon,

nor, across her darkened hips,

the scatters

of bright yellow gorse.

Ed Lyons

Notes on New Mexico, the Land of Enchantment, and its Ancient City of Taos

It's that kind of weather after the rain:
Cool and sunny, clouds of brilliant white;
The rivers fall back to their banks again,
And I recall that clear and golden light
Coming over the ridge out of the night
In springtime when the cottonwoods are green
I recall a place where we have been

Where sage grows over a hundred mile plain,
Sweet sap and otherworldly smoke that fills
Adobe rooms; upon a silver chain,
The crystals, beads and jewels. A wind flute trills
Its song of birds and spirits of the hills.
The junipers grow through the lava stones
Along the canyon, and the dried-out bones

Of cattle on the dry and rocky ground
That people find and hang upon the walls,
The dark and lovely faces, and the sound
Of the sacred river that from the mountain falls
Down through the Pueblo, the emptiness that calls
Through the depths on dark and silent wings:
I think of these and a thousand other things.

On a highway somewhere west of Amarillo
(Matchbox city, toy highway, trucks and cars)
She was exhausted, dozing on her pillow,
(Somewhere between Oklahoma and the stars
We'd driven all night) the Grateful Dead's guitars
Twined in secret rivers of vines, and I
Glimpsed the silver object in the sky,

Which took me back to color-coded dreams
    About a rainbow flowering in the spine
And time stood still beyond the withered streams
    And sage, and reddish stone; the vine
    Grew lush within my thoughts, and I felt fine
So many hours past the need for sleep,
Somewhere west of Tucumcari, in the deep

Rangelands where the red escarpments tear
    Upward from the sunken riverbed,
Wondering, what the thought that put this there,
    Feeling kind of crazy in the head,
    Driving, listening to the Grateful Dead,
And when we reached the top the mountains rose
Above our heads, specked with the late snows

Of spring, the towns with Spanish names:
    Las Vegas, Mora, at five, then ten
Then seven thousand feet, the yellow flames
    Like arrows from a visionary sun
    (and think of all of that as it had been:
The tipis circled in the sun or snow,
Unfettered herds of sacred buffalo,

Rattlesnakes and drums and prairie flowers
    And herds of antelope, and endless gold,
And blue horizon hills like waves, the powers
    Of the four directions, the winds unfold.
    Enter the mind of life, let it take hold,
The mind of the Great Spirit, and all creation's
Perfect circle, harmony of all relations).

Ed Lyons

Lady Liberty

Lines written upon seeing Jefferson Starship Perform
across the River from Philadelphia

She dreamed she was a sparrow in the twilight,
a butterfly, a river in the air—
She thought I was an arrow in the daylight,
I dreamed I was a flower in her hair,
In daylight calling, falling through the river:
The singer and the giver.

A thousand days, a thousand years of nighttime,
And legends told of battlefield and storm—
She touched me in the solitude of dreamtime,
In solitude the dream took shape and form.
At dawn I saw her walking in the garden:
The flowers were her children.

She traveled in the mountains in the moonlight
In liquid seasons when the time was gold,
And her eyes were golden in the firelight.
Like the sun I watched her life unfold,
And I could hear the breathing of an angel
Upon a sea of crystal.

* * *

I think there are a million answers
And these
Oceans and oceans of silence
That burn
Between the fair horizon
And the freedom that once held me in thrall.

I think there are a million questions
That indicate
The time is upon us
When we must discern
Between the dreams that feed us
And the things
We only dreamed
In restlessness, discomfort, and despair.

And this is the Revolution!
You should not hesitate
To reach deep within
Your precious spirit
To find your way through the troubles
That deceive you in your darkest hour!

This is the Victory!
I will not hesitate
To lend myself
To this new beginning,
This new tremendous
Reaching for the dawn!

* * *

She was the kind of woman I could live for,
    She was a flaming flower in my soul,
She's Lady Liberty – and through the door
    Of infinite tomorrows the waters roll
    Like thunder through the brilliant seas of love--
                                        She's what I'm thinking of.

Now History is Dead

Spring came with a vengeance. The hills are green
  And green the forests, green the boughs that hang
Over city streets, and gray the rain
  And mist and mountains. We heard the bells that rang
Over avenues and parks and in
  Our ears, every wavelength, visible
    And invisible, harmonious
As the wind and sea, and worlds within,
  A vision gaining force, becoming feasible;
    My thoughts scattered on the wind melodious.

And all the planet sings, the tension, joy,
  Gathers to its critical intensity –
Waves, spirals, loving, girl and boy
  Forged in fiery circles, electricity
Wings across the ocean like tachyon eagles,
  The eagle and the condor in their soaring
    Over the thunder-studded Caribbean,
And the people, lost in tiresome struggles
  Awaken to the fire that is roaring
    Within the mind of God. You are forgiven

No matter what you think you did to whom,
  No matter what the television says
To make you think your body is the tomb
  Where nothing but your inadequacy lies –
Don't believe that for a minute, sister, brother!
  the truth is, we are one being!
    One perfect circle, drawing to a close.
Lost, we find our home in one another,
  Out of darkness, in dawn, the first time seeing
    The whole mandala of the mystic rose.

Know who you are. That's all that matters.
  In darkness, fed on lies, that's where we've been.
The ugly world of yesterday that shatters
  All around us, that said you're full of sin,
You're ugly. Or you're stupid, or whatever,
  Lacks power to enforce its greedy claims.
    Arise, my love, be beautiful and free!
And who you are, full of love forever.
  The devil and the government he blames
    Are broken, and you are allowed to be.

So rise up then, you glorious Andean soul,
  Beyond the Kansas plains, of liberty
Sings out like the summer storms that roll
  Through the Southern night. Monotony
Of time, of hours, minutes, that old chain
  Restrains us no more: the debt's invalid.
    Our lives were paying what was never real.
I'm standing naked in the summer rain.
  If I can think it, it must be allowed.
    I'm sorry, friends, that's just the way I feel.

If I Tell the Truth

I wasn't always honest
It was all about perspective
the silent space of muted tongue
a 'yes' to presumption.
How one sees Rapunzel
Protected, or snared?

I was like an old worn shoe, how
it curves into the shape of feet,
contoured your desperation.
I'd watched my father, learned
his skill: natural rock, piled in layers,
roughened slab, each piece unique,
each answering to the master's eye,
making stone walls a craft.

I didn't crochet like my mother, but knew
how to catch your hook, thread deceptions
into lace, stitch, mend, plait fabrications,
seam my shawl.

Birds who fly must return to earth,
in the garden, a wood pigeon,
industrious, makes her nest.
Tolerance knows,
we all evolve, from someone's family,
and you were part of mine.

Despondency

Arrived, an unwelcome visitor,
a hungry heron, unsure of prey.
A dark cloud filled the air.
At first glance I could not see,
slate eyes penetrate
empty places. Sound,

a vibration, like a crow
cawing before rain.
Now I welcome its company,
We spoke, I listened, chatted
about necessary loss, the things

I loved,
pictures, trips, that china cup
and him, the importance of
grief in letting go.
Peace moved in. After,
we made tea, dunked biscuits.

This dark cloak, my friend,
its pockets.

Togher, Tuam Co. Galway: September 1987

I don't want to forget you,
*my invisible one with no nam*e,
the warm clench of you will not die,
even in the claw of death.

I will not forget
I was making bread when you came away,
first a dart, a knife forced up between my legs,
spears slashed my vulva,
spikes jabbed into visceral skin.

I will not forget
the sting, a lance cutting my womb,
wrenched, tearing flesh, feet to heart,
my silent scream, my breath a blade.

I will not forget
how trickles of blood streamed in lines,
one after another down my legs,
long red tears pooled over my shoes,
clasped to stop the bleeding.

I will not forget
how alone I felt, like late at night
in a dark field, blinding tears, my dry mouth.
You were coming away, tearing loose, a volume
of clots gushed, lumps of jelly, weight in my groin.

I will not forget
getting to the bathroom, my inflamed rickety body,
white bowl splattered in red, floor a mass
of ruddy splashes, crimson paper, bloodied towel.

Attracta Fahy

Will not forget
I bundled drenched tissues into stove,
fire flared in orange, yellow flames,
dried black on my tongue,

I will not forget
when it stopped, rushed to doctor,
'test still positive,' he said, 'came away clean,'
'complete abortion,' his medical term,
the tiled floor no comfort.

I will not forget
I didn't know you existed.

I will never forget
my return, the bleak of kitchen, desolate home,
half made dough, not knowing
if you'd flushed or burned, guilt crawled
like a rat over my skin.

Out through the window, rolling
green fields, cows mother their calves,
sheep with their lambs.
I wanted to feel the soft of your skin,
its silk breeze on my face, your colour,
eyes, hair. I wanted to have
your storms, rain, thunder, your smile.
I wanted even the dead of you.

No, I will not forget your existence,
All that labour without knowing, holding,
whoever you were.

I will not forget
when I told him, he said, washing his hands,
'How did that happen?' 'I don't know,' I replied,
'Is there any dinner?'
We never spoke of you again.

How I Hold Back Monsters

There's something always standing behind me;
An indefinite humanoid shape,
Aura gray to greenish-black.
Even when I'm sitting with my back to a wall,
The way I am now, I know it's bending its head
At an unnatural angle
To read over my shoulder, peering at the screen,
Or to ogle through my eyes, greedy,
And reaching out with an appendage
From behind my back toward the panorama;
I wonder if the touch of its gray-green skin
Would cause plants or people to wither.
I don't want life to wither as I watch.
I would restrain my familiar with magic,
But I don't know any spells for that,
Besides I think it would know what I was doing
And with one caress of its cloudy digits on my spine
Make me shiver my life out through all my orifices.
Obviously I can't physically banish it.
It might be that I can combat it
With an expression of pure will;
Turn around and face it,
Look into the hollow spaces that might be eyes
And refuse it power over my real reality;
But turning around merely means I'm facing the wall
And the figure is still behind me,
Out in the panorama now,
Floating out in the parking lot,
Running its hand, if it is a hand, over a windshield
And seeming more solid in the ambient exhaust.
When I turn around again,
It leans half out of the wall.

So I let it bend its insubstantial head
Over my shoulder, reading what I write;
If it seems pleased, that's an unreliable impression.
One of many.

Anne McMaster

Lost and Found

inspired by Robert MacFarlane's *The Lost Words*

You may think we have misplaced these living words only for a moment -
as one might, casually, lose a small, cool coin
behind the sofa – or drop a sweet that melts into a sticky mass
in the corner of that pocket of our favourite coat.
Objects some time lost then gladly found. But this is so much more.
We first forget the shape of the word in our very mouth –
the thick curve of tongue pressed against teeth.
Pursed lips stretching to shape now unfamiliar syllables;
spitting words out like rough, unworn pebbles
that fall into dead air flat beside our feet.
Then we forget their meanings -
– these words that tied us to our moments in the natural world;
our memories, our seasons and our way of life.
A door quietly closes. A light gradually dims.
Before we know, both the explanation and the experience -
the meaning and the moment - are gone.
To lose these precious words
is to lose stories that should be both our connection
and our currency – our link to the present and the past.
Share these words even now. Seek to explain and
to understand. Offer them generously to others
like a strange, familiar fruit that blossoms in hidden corners, still.
Taste them so that we may remember.
Taste them so that we may not forget.

Shelby Stephenson

One House: One Person

Comes the time when it's five
and the fridge's door's alive
with Samuel Adams and Peroni.
I choose Peroni.

I learned that it,
the beer, I mean, does fit
the bulbous bow of the *SS Rex*,
that ocean liner of the classical deck.

I'm serious: a beer
by any other fame would be a deer
or a dog old-fashioned
as my mother's dachshund.

Honestly, I open the door,
wondering if my friend Carol
ever was a passenger.
The thought opens a can of challengers.

Carol travels a lot.
Though the ship was hit by rockets
in 1944, caught on fire and burned,
I still like to picture Italy's cultural emergence.

I love luxury, not war.
Myths and legends I adore.
That's why I open the door
of my Whirlpool Frigidaire –

Slowly. I take one Blue Riband
Peroni and pour it in a glass decorated
with frost from the freezer.
The first sip cures my cabin fever.

Toti O'Brien

Joan of Arc

And if myth is the thing you eat for breakfast
stale bread soaked in milk
plastic cup of faded green

And if fair is the flip side of what burns under your sternum
when you feel you have been wronged
but how, you can't tell

In the cellar, where you have been shut
in order to meditate on your sins
you sip bitter swags of angst and revolt

If unfair has nothing to do with justice or rights
only with a knot in your throat
that causes your gagging
*
Suddenly, as rage's eating your chest
you are climbing a ladder
your wrist ringed by the sweaty grip of mute fingers

Fair has nothing to do with kind
like your missing mother
or with blond and light-skinned

Only with a noise beyond the smothering hush
of your blindfold, a crowd witnessing
your blame and your shame

Unaware of the vain, vague rebellion
making you into their laughing stock
their thrill

Their attraction that is just a distraction
to relieve endless tedium
and the vacancy of gods
*
Dusty wind pricks the skin of your nape
the pink strip between ear and scalp
freshly shaven

Itchy like the brush
you stroke on the back
of your darling mare

In the stable, that's where you belong
or else in the kitchen
but the hand you can't see holds you tighter
*
In a somnambulic daze
you sense smoke
and the heat of a distant summer

(Sun scorching your freckled cheeks
in an open field
remote innocence)

Your heart throbs
while your jailer crushes your bones
as if squeezing lymph out of a twig

You are the kindling
to your own holocaust
Slowly, you become myth

Saltwater

An Gorta Mór

Sixteen years old and saved from the workhouse,
her coffin ship exile crossed an Atlantic gulf,
a terrifying space on a trail of dying
dropped to the depths of an empire's throat.

Only once, during months of hunger and fever
as her siblings slipped into funeral spray,
she allowed a drop of saltwater
to reach the roof of her mouth.
She held it there till the end of her days,
never swallowing, never spitting it out.

Michael J. Whelan

Communion

Oldbawn, Tallaght – prior to the lockdown

This is a poem
from a suburban back garden,
midsummer in Dublin 2019,
to slow the world down.

Fly over here little blue butterfly
so we will know we are not alone.
Come little robin, rest your wings next to my chair,
turn your head to explore me as you did each morning,
when the sun warmed my arms and legs.

Deep time occurs,
a thousand years of living in this city,
I feel them, people of the past,
vanished from this place - these streets they knew,
the tall, shaped skies they built.
We see them in the movie reels, moving quickly,
fleeting moments of flesh and blood
looking back at us curiously
from their foreign country.
Where have they all gone?
the graveyards don't seem deep enough.

No sun blazed heat-wave like last year,
still, I'm sitting under an open parasol waiting for it,
my frame filling the cave entrance into the bushes
where I know the robin's always build their nest.
I can hear their chick above the pitch of a low flying jet –

holiday makers on their way to the *paid for* sun.
I can even hear the cupped sound of lilies as they fall on the ground.

A robin has landed beside me – an insect gripped tightly in its beak,
she studies me - I like to think, or maybe I'm just blocking her path.
She tilts her head, she is beautiful, and I tilt mine in response every time –
our simple communion.

Every few seconds wings flutter, my heart flutters, the parasol creaks
like the rigging of a coffin ship, the timber decks of an old schooner
whispering of passages to a promised new world.

Sparrows splash in the birdbath as if there's no tomorrow, creating waves,
I left food on the table for them earlier.
Solstice comes with the breeze in its feathers –
an old heron observing new rain from a neighbour's roof
moving quickly from the west, he keeps the wisdom of Earth's
rotation and all our days growing shorter.

I determine to wait here and see what happens, to feed the universe
with birdseed while summertime exists.

Trish Bennett

Border Child

I come from bogs and butchers, reared
on a diet of rumour in a small kitchen, heated
by the polished copper-pipe range.
I come from a childhood of fields, rivers and lanes
where my friends and I cycled our bikes,
as we freewheeled towards freedom.
I come from cocoa before bed each night, reading
under cover of flashlight, being haunted
by stories of banshees and bogeymen.
I come from a place shaken by bombs, surrounded
by a river that sliced into them and us,
the bridges between — blocked by barricades.
I come from patrols, searches, red strobes
under cover of night, suspicion
at cars parked on lonely roads.
I come from adults being polite
to the flashlight in their face, for fear
of bogeymen in the ditches.

Innisfree, Me Arse!
(Sincere apologies to W.B.)

Small cabins are not ideal,
a king size bed, an island kitchen,
they'll never fit in.
Clay and wattle's all well and good
but you're better with the block.
Insulate like the Swedes,
for the Autumn wind whips across that lake,
skins ash and beech,
to cover paths, and fill the gutters,
brings with it Canadian Geese, who come
to keep you up all night,
with their honk-bonk orgy by the shore.
Skeletal cats move in,
take over chairs and laps,
purring and pats,
turn into big brutes that drag in prey
and lap milk night and day
with low sounds by the door.
Linnets won't get a look in
with the magpies and the crows,
who sit in trees
to Gogglebox your windows like reality TV,
as they wait to steal the food you leave
for tits.

For evenings filled with wings,
get an African Grey.
He'll dive bomb dinner with a kaw and a kak,
shout ME ARSE!
throwing scraps to the dog
— barking mad.
Don't plant the nine bean rows,

for steroid-pumped slugs
— the size of an ink stained thumb,
will scoff your hopeful shoots.
As for slug traps filled with stout,
those louts'll down the lot,
then slime home on beer bellies
lost in the plot.

If you love Game of Thrones,
get that hive of honey bees.
The summer's filled with battles,
and drones in death throes
after mating with the queen,
Poor lads, they come
— as they go.
A bee loud glade's not the place to live alone,
for it's far from cricket song
when you dangle at an angle
on a ladder saying prayers,
as you cut a branch of brown winged leaves
that breaks to a roar,

and a swarm of twenty thousand bees
drop slow,
into a cardboard box,
balanced on the head
of your only help
— a passing ten-year-old.
Walkers stroll down your road
on their way to the shore,
stand to admire the birds and the bees
in your gardens flowering trees.
They don't notice the cats
giving death-stares from below,

'til your little dog barks
RIP THEIR HEADS OFF!,
and your Grey
wolf-whistles like a sailor out the door.
I hope they feel your peace
in their deep heart's core.

NOTE:
"Innisfree, Me Arse!," is my response to the 'Lake Isle of Innisfree', one of my favourite poems by WB Yeats. I've lived in Sligo in my student years and often visit family there. I've toured Lough Gill and went for walks in Hazelwood and feel a strong connection to his words. As a result I've written several poems in response to his lines. When I found my own Innisfree, a small house by the lake, planted the bean rows and got the hive of honey bees, I realised what a dreamer Yeats really was.

Another Reply to Merwin

The soul is such that
It is lost in the keeping,
Its growth achieved
by giving it away
and while you're making
That small gift
(for the soul is smaller
than you might imagine)
if you're afraid of losing
it, the danger is that fear,
for the soul has an advantage,
O infinite division,
which cannot be
what you were worried about.
It is not, after all, merely
yourself you are giving,
Only that eternal part
you were left with
From the beginning.

Always There

You gave me the sunset,
neatly wrapped in a flaming cloth
with golden ribbons lacing its warmth.
I can rest tonight,
knowing tomorrow will rise with me.

I hear your call through foggy windows and
know you hold my hand to gather strength,
before your cinnamon brown wings sail on to
find another song, or two, or three,
that you'll nestle and cherish until our next meet.

The air I breathe will wrap
my aching body in fresh life,
full of hope that I'll carry with me.
As the day's troubles gather,
you never leave my side.

Julie Stevens

Chasing Rain

If I step outside
the wind will drag me this way and that,
the clouds will roar at me and soak me in chasing rain,
the air will be shrieking my fear, whilst shadowing every step.

If I step outside
my footsteps will stare down a broken paving slab,
my ears will locate the passers-by framed together,
my legs will be weighed down by every question.

But if I stay inside
the wolves will chase me from room to room,
the fear flies will find me and scavenge my stomach,
whilst the thought tigers will cage me and lock the door.

My carefully crafted balance has been shaken
everything trapped in this anxious storm,
I'm frantically searching for my book of perfect choices,
my umbrella of peace needs opening.

Kari Flickinger

I Wandered into a Beehive

I wandered into a beehive
in manzanita. Ten-year-old in red
turtleneck sweater, like a specific
children's book cat on her first
day of school. The stinging mass
attached. Vicious. But, today

I wish I had more scarf to cover my
neck and mouth. Stay the breath. Stay
inside keep the air from expulsion. Not
the droning. I would give you more

explanation. See, sometimes you pulse
in and out and I am falling back
in love with myself. It's not good enough
to excuse the effort expended; especially
when love has built hive mind and a mess
is how our honey fastens. I didn't think

because I'd heard
even after centuries, in a cask mouldering
in a pyramid, honey will still
flow. Honey, but I know you, can add
the right bugs to make an alcoholic.
Under this thin skin, I'm gutted by bees
flying back through time.

How do I tell you I'm still that stung
child, wandering lost in a puzzle maze of manzanita?

Kari Flickinger

Branches. Roots.

the wind just lifted
the branches outside my sliver of window.
my heart is broken.
the most brilliant beautiful woman I have ever known just died.

She-of-constant
bloom-filled kitchen
enfolds, says

you're lucky

when I tell her I am
studying what she is

living. Bulbs

crinkle at the ends. She
flips from blue bright

surprise. Feathers near
translucent in her delicate
lap rest, inactive.

Her chin yields a fine
crop of protective hairs

I want to reach out

to trace along this
furry slope I have

memorized since
opening my first

book. Reaching pulp.
Scrabble board. Soft

boiled egg. Two
porcelain pigs

on this kitchen
shelf above her boughs.

These wounds used to
thrive, discover, fingerprint.

I crumble to stars as she pats
my knee. Stops.

Stares at the wall
behind me. Art

has flown; her instructive
smile is replaced by

a lack. Her spark

no longer aflame; the chill
has come and she has fallen
from her branch.

Coyote Howling
for Melanie Diana

3 am: In the late September woods, a coyote
howling deep within the trees snaps me out of sleep.
The sound seems mournful, dark, a human voice in
need, someone loved and lost, or fear at one's own
end. I wonder, is there a message there for me?

I recall coyotes when I lived out West and saw them
running over fields, along the roads, lean and scruffy,
quick to disappear. But driving through that country,
even in the night, I never heard one howl.

What I hear tonight reminds me of a song my father
used to sing about three children left in the woods
to die. Had they been abandoned by their parents,
the secret fear of every child? Perhaps the ancient
German tribes were right to name their forest Black.

But remembering coyotes act the Trickster,
I reevaluate the message: Is the woeful howl urging
just the opposite of fear and ruin? Could it be a call
to see beyond the trees that block the ordered light
of stars and hide the steady solace of the moon?

So I think of autumn's gold and crimson, then the
reassuring grey of winter trees, and in spring, green
shoots pushing through the litter of last year's leaves,
then summer's warm abundance. And now comes
dawn, renewing everything.

Elegy in A Minor Key

for Jay Hoffman

The year or day you died
or how, are still not clear to me,
despite my dogged reverence
for history, except I learned
"by his own hand," a phrase
that could be heard as judgement,
or simply cold and distancing,
without such saving knowledge
of the desperate loss
that took you to whatever
sort of end it was, or when.
I have no metaphor for
stepping deftly past your pain
because I really haven't known
It's kind. Yet I still need
to recognize your life's
brief passage over mine.

We shared poetry and laughs,
nights in smoky bars,
as well as wonder, longing too,
you telling of the lights at night
across the harbor at Kowloon,
me standing on a fragile bluff
above the brown Missouri
surging wildly in the spring,
and all that seasoned in a sense
of the absurd and sometimes
sullen nature of our lives.

But mostly I remember
you were kind enough
to buy another round
and listen to my song.

cooking lesson

after "Cooking." by Gertrude Stein

alas a lass Alice at last the eye pulls from its little leaf
a seed not yet put in soil to multiply swell fill out get
taller the ear heeds the call hears the bell shuns the stall
coached from its lazy couch what china this receptacle
what better meat than mollusk a whole community in bed
together sperm wedded into water the muscular feet one
each per shell propelling the premises scant regard for logic

Nuances

nuances...
the hidden obvious
the in-betweens
the fine print that everyone sees
yet does not read
hearing hints like canine whistles in intimate distance
but don't pause in the details to regard

and respond

those

senses like smells
faint
but strong

those specifics

little foxes that can ruin
if unchecked
or

the heart language

even the dialect

found in the simplistic and the depth

the quiet movements of communication that each one desires to be noticed...

...and honored

the hope for empathetic exchange
the follow and leading and walking in the dot connections

the agreement in the breath within, Sẹlah...

the care of holy perceptions

(perceiving our beings and relationship as holy ground where God dwells)
the receiving and speaking of sacred thoughts that words cannot say
just knowing

and walking in the
"Ok"

the freedom of yes

fruitful awareness
manifestation of keenness
living His prayer of oneness

answering Him in the steps...

relationship of three
me
Him

you = We
Engrafted into seamless
Love being the constant

Ever-Filling and

unfolding
by jot and title covenant decision.

Beneath the Blue Soil

When a world forgets
looks at its own reflection
thoughts on reaching the end –
resurfacing in the middle of the night;
we watched the shoreline move
its barbarous scenes of swaying light;
a man walks into the sea.
Skin as white as Japanese seabass
he has not come to swim tonight –
jeans hanging from crooked pine
pale shirt stiffened by sea air
blowing in the wind like war-torn flags -
a man walks into the sea.
blue soil washing against face -
wedding ring stitched
inside the stomach of a crab.

Matt Duggan

We Have Done Our Best to Break Mother

Watching the rain on a slant
like a cat staring through glass
awaiting that moment of release;

where we grew into our chains
– & each one chronicled
the breakdown in four parts;

If we held shadows far from us
in our minds curled up
like children we once were.

When spiked trees danced
threw ghosts into burial clouds -
the wind inside uncertain skies
became a sculptor of our hell & fantasy.

We have done our best to break mother
filled her sea with blood & oils
scattered the residue of plastic containers
along her shoreline in triplets & two's.

Hand of the dead

mama's wedding band
on my ring finger
sister's diamond on my pinky
got it from her children
to remember her
as if I could forget

papa's wedding band
on the pointer
he hardly wore it
for fear it would get caught
in the machinery he operated

I found it in a jewelry box
next to mama's bracelet
now on my wrist
the one papa bought for her
on her birthday

rings and bracelet
adorn my hand
reminders
of the profound legacy
I wear inside my heart

Mali Warshofsky

Crows

the squeal of crows
startles the calm silence
of a gentle summer day

shrilling cries pierce
a blue expanse

crows transform
the luscious green treetops
to black nervous chaos

Preparing to Return

Her clothes hung in a musty wardrobe
long after the smell of perfume had faded.

The remnants of her life; boxes of baby tags
and old photographs to which we now turn.

On top, a savings book, insurance policy,
and grave papers for a child not spoken of,
to whom she was preparing to return.

Karen Mooney

Adrift

Packed, sealed, pitched into a swell of hope.
Fragile exterior chipped. Inside, sodden
with salty water that rises like the tide.

Adrift in an ocean where boundaries
are belittled and challenged
by each incoming surge.
It will not be denied.

Washed up on strange shores,
debris to some, incarcerated
among rocks, shells, sand and kelp.
Message stained, partly pulped,
barely legible.

A translation of experience
impossible to understand,
hoping to blend in,
yearning to be released.

Who will lift me up, hold me, take time
to unpick the seal, let me dry out?
Who will look into salt-crusted circles
to see the depths to which I've been plunged?

David Atkinson

Stone-walling

I never want to be a brick;
six sides, twelve edges,
eight corners, and whilst coming
in different sizes, they are,
in essence, all the same;
clay and water, compression and heat,
laid end to end, top to tail,
whole houses built on their heads.

I want to be Mourne granite, Antrim basalt,
plucked from a field and carefully placed
with other stones of all shapes and sizes,
held together by our differences,
proud to be part of a wall the wind
whistles through, rather than around.

Janet Barbaritz

In the Dirt

Mark of his desire
He aims not for her affection
But her song
Far more dear

She is not
A maiden of careless pulchritude
And tousled hair
But a competitor

Ready to wrestle
In bare feet with gritted teeth
On hallowed ground
And win

Janet Barbaritz

And then

they bring lantern blooms from the park
and the steamy breath of an asphalt walk
surrounded by woods

that cooks the low country boil
ever more quickly
tender potatoes and corn

and he brings out Sunday plates
and I add spearmint to the tea
while little dog's eyes flutter and close

Wendy Holborow

After The Silent Phone Call
(i.m. my parents, Lynn and Dwynwen)

After the silent phone call
our daughter dries my tears,
paper lanterns litter our lives.
My son pyramids used teabags.
A wintry sun throws prisms
on the pair of terraria
planted with ivy and African
violets - violence shadows my prison.

Princess purrs to the newly born
in the shower-tray, despatching me
to wallow in the bath.
A storm swallows the light,
bulls bellow its arrival, ducks
& geese in serried rows
hypnotised by the storm's eye,
grey mare merges into greyness
of fogged rain-soaked field.
Cowering dogs return with nonchalance,
with unconditional love as calm
is restored. I vainly count
days not to be crushed
in the house at the
end of the axle-breaking track.

Walking in walled autumnal gardens,
trees like antlered animals rear
into the sky. Gathering fruit
for wine, sloes for gin
inebriation sets in. I forage
for mushrooms, the magic ones,
imagination soars, friends, fairy-tale end.

Carelessly, people slip through craquelure
in paintings of imagined lives.
Great clouds plough straight furrows,
confront coffins at open graves.
Lynn's smoking extinguishes his life.
Dwynwen (Welsh goddess of love)
her chocolate heart cracks, flakes
and Fiona is brutally murdered.

(I wish I'd told her
of the solitary snowdrop
that grew on the grave
of the dog she loved.)

Shipwrecked Sun

Shipwrecked the sun
sinks
into the snatching sea
in all its tangled colours:
blood red / yellow / orange /
spangled scarlet / magenta /

the sagging gales of grief
toss the wreck of sun
around the hapless waves
that arch and crash
into smithereens
smothering the shrieks of gulls

but not the cries of my wild lament
at the loss of you from my life
the loss that wrecked my soul
where there is no escape from grief.

The shipwrecked sun
submerges
fully below
the leaping sea

which tires, breathes,
becomes calm, shuffles to the shore

Death Was a Wind and A Flood

It came in the night
and it came in the light.

It broke the children and their parents,
the mothers who smiled
and the fathers who worked in the fields.

Death broke them
and buried them
and scattered dust
over their graves
and told a story
about death
and the road it takes
to heaven.

The dead wept
and nodded and listened
and wrote their own stories down
and kept them close to their hearts.

They knew a story was hope.

Dying

My father said he would never die.
He said he had never died
and there was no proof
that he would ever die.

When his time came
from the liver cancer
that would finally kill him,
he fought it as hard
as he ever fought the Nazis
in Buchenwald.

The doctors and nurses
strapped him to the hospital bed
because -- even though
he couldn't even stand --
he was determined
to walk out of the hospital
and go home.

Patty Cole

Watermelon Miracles and Pink Cotton Fairytales

Delores yells from the kitchen,
The weatherman on the news keeps
telling me it's going to get up to 105
today. But the TV's broken and I wonder
what she's doing in the kitchen—if
she took her meds.

Only the foolish, barks Delores up the stairs.
Her cigarette smoke finds my nose. Hachooo!
She means only a fool would go out in 105-degree heat.
I guess I won't be going to the pool today.
Can I go to the pool today?

Lord, I guess, but all you get is an hour.
I want you in this house by 10 o'clock.
Man, something changed in her overnight
because today she is living in *my* world.

Delores giving me orders tastes sweet like
a watermelon, something I want every day
and not just when a miracle happens, as when
she wakes out of her Thorazine stupor and
is all pretty to us, which only happens
on Thanksgiving and on Christmas,
when she has to.

But today Delores is taking charge
the way a mom would, the way my
next-door-neighbor-friend Amy's mom does.
Amy's curfew may be too strict but she has
someone who cares where she is.

Delores, a skinny, blonde with big blue eyes,
hollers: *bacon and eggs on the stove,*
cantaloupe and orange juice on the table.
But she doesn't have to say so; the smell of

bacon frying and her voice are enough for me
to believe she is my Mom and I am her prisoner.

I wonder if Dad noticed anything different
in Delores before he went to the school
to arrange music for band camp.
Like does he know how hot it's going to get?

I'm gonna jump back in bed and make Delores
call me for breakfast again. *I mean it*, she says.
I get to hear her talk to me again.
When she does I feel a mother's love wrap around
my entire body the way this pink cotton blanket I got
for my 15th birthday does.

Whenever I cover myself, head to toe, I enter a
fairytale where Delores is a Fairytale Mom
with a wand to fix every broken thing in
our broken lives. I imagine her bandaging my scrapes,
brushing my hair, fussing over my make-up and the
way my clothes fit, kissing my cheek. It all sparkles.

When I'm at the kitchen table I swing my legs, like-sassy-like,
to show I have what Amy has, meals that never stop.
I reach for Mom's hand putting mine on hers.
She doesn't move. Instead, she stares at something
or someone next to the refrigerator. Ghosts. Spirits.
This house is getting *too* crowded.

Delores leaves everything out in the kitchen
with the stove on and a burning cigarette
on the edge of the table. A dazed zombie, she goes
to the den to sit, smoke, stare, frown, and laugh
so hard tears pour off her face.

Now I know I'd better stay home today.
It's already too hot.

Patty Cole

Barbie Dolls and Big-Girl Bras

I remember the first day of seventh grade.
I was somewhere between Donnie Osmond
and Saturday Night Fever, Barbie dolls
and big-girl bras waiting my turn
for the old, bent-up merry-go-round
on the playground behind our school building
originally used by third graders.

Kids clung to the spinning ride as it hummed
against late summer with its saturating smell
of cut turf from the football field.
I wanted to be part of the group, young enough
to enjoy remnants of recess, old enough to realize
we were riding memories.

Then midair in front of me, he leaned
over the slowing ride. His head was a
jack-o-lantern—fiery eyes, crooked smile—
suspended as if hanging by a thread.
He spat onto my right shin. The playground
burst into laughter, faces crimped in impish cheer.

In the restroom, I rubbed the spot with a
wet paper towel until it hurt.
Girls side-stepped behind me laughing
as they sang snarky quatrains.

The entire morning was a blur:
spit, laughter, mocking faces.

Did I cry that day?
I can't remember that.

Andy Oram

Roster

The default gender is male

The default language is English

The default city for poetic edge is New York

The default shirt size is large

The default home heating is natural gas

The default gun caliber is twenty-two

The default mode of death among young black men is homicide

The default asylum status is denied

The default lines fissure gape engulfs

For we do not admit our defaults, we do not atone

Too bad there's no default god

Andy Oram

1. **No longer**

An acceptable response no longer:

Torpor has been struck from the catalog

Grocery stores are cleared of decaf coffee—

They want us to stay awake at this time

The climes call us outside—

Planting season in the Northern hemisphere and crisp Autumn in the South

As for that Roku

It should be put into its own torpor every once in a while

I feel that I'm waiting in a dusk-decked vestibule

As if for the gates of the locks to open—for a

Gust of spirit that channels the suppressed joys of the nations   I am waiting for time capsules to open

For their contents to start up a chant

2. We don't ask when that house will sell

Behind the streaked windows nothing's there

No corners—it's too dark for them
No memories—too moldy

Just swirls of dust

Where sofas and end tables lay long ago.

Tracks too—

On the ceilings, drips from disrespectful pipes
On the walls, grease from irresponsible diners

Heedless tacks tear holes in the plaster through which
The passions of decades escape and wheeze into the neighborhood atmosphere.

The grass remains cut, only because the bank sends someone.

If you were to violate this no-man's land and peek inside for discards,

No dog would bark.
No envelopes have prodded out from the mailbox for months.
No nieces stop by to leave biscotti or soup pots on the porch.

Nobody ever gets off the 6:24 bus

That stops on week nights at a faded aluminum marker before the
    house.
Up and down the pavement, parents call in
The basketballs and jump ropes before dark.
  Walk the street between one sad face and another.
  You will know why no one moves into this house.

Tonight the figure of a cat can be glimpsed under one of the working street lamps,

    Not needing to bed down in the home from which it strayed,
    Because it is starting to find its biggest prey.

Peach Delphine

When you sleep without pain

Light lies dusty
in the road, as mourning doves
summon sunrise, still a spilled candle
smoking on the horizon,

so many small birds
flower in our mouths,
a wind of railroad vine
blanket flower rattles cabbage palms.

Sky empty as lightning whelks
sun bleached, sands
gathered, poured
into jars, azure hammered

thin as foil, moon
of broken sand dollar
dim, distant.
Day gathers momentum,

you hold this form as if warmth
was a garment shared between us
as if pain was not stitched
into your breathing
as if today implies tomorrow
or conch held the sound of sea,
always the sea, each wave a text

song unfolded from hands
taking flight then vanishing
tide abandons creek
tide abandons mangrove

we stand derelict, waterless,
darkness of eyes, darkness of clouds
flowing off the Gulf,
lamps will not light this place

as cerulean yields to burgundy
as night folds us into velvet,
when we sleep
you sometimes hold my hand

as if to keep me from floating
away on a current felt but unseen,
sometimes the simplest touch
is all we have,

the smallest flower
all the vine can sustain
the smallest word
uttered in darkness

A geisha, at a military reception on the Tokkaido, speaks to my grandfather, a Calvinist missionary

Sir, you say
the meek are blessed. You say
the pure in heart will see God. You say
if we suffer for Him we shall
earn a place in His kingdom.
I say
this afternoon the mountain is lying
there on the west horizon. At its base—
do you see them? —a row of
tiny houses. In this small wind
their walls shiver. In a great wind
they'll disappear.
Sir, do you see
the children chasing their kites? Do you hear
in the wind somewhere a woman singing,
plucking her strings?
Here below us
the sea is pale, pebbly water, not
deep blue. The sails—out there
and there and there—are bleached white, not
the color of a tangerine. And yet
just now, in this first light of sunset,
please look at them.

China

One man on the bridge,
worth its weight in silver.
Two men on the bridge,
worth its weight in gold.
Three men, my Mother whispered,
priceless.

She cradled
a bowl between her hands.
Three men's the oldest.

And pointed
to tiny figures sketched
in the smooth blue and white porcelain
her grandfather's grandfather
brought back from Canton
in his three-mast ship,
stowed under silks and tea.

From the 1820's on,
no men. Just the peak-roof house
where the merchant's daughter lived,
the willow tree, the bare bridge,
the shallop of the young prince
sailing up the river toward
hills on the far horizon.

Did the painters get lazy?
Did they say to each other
Why would the foreigners care?

Then came the Opium Wars.
The death of the Dragon Empress.
The Great Leap Forward.

The passing of my Mother,
who must have known
the story of the three men.

Nastashia Minto

Breathe

I don't know which way to breathe.
If I should put my hands up or behind my back.
Is it going to be covid-19 or a gun man that lays me flat?

I don't know which way to breathe.
Because through my nose seems problematic.
Eric Gardner was asthmatic
Tamir rice had fake pellets
And Sandra bland they'll never tell us.

So I don't know which way to breathe.
Because every time I un-tense my jaw
relax my shoulders I see another dead brown body on TV.

I don't know which way to breathe.
They hear the unintelligent slang from the south.
I have to what the tone from my mouth.
I'll keep my button-ups for the streets
And leave the hoodies for the house.

I don't know which way to breathe.
Or should I leave that for the ventilators.
Police said this is a closed casket.
DOA they didn't even try to resuscitate them.

I don't know which way to breathe.
Will I have enough oxygen in my blood to oxygenate me?

My lungs are shaped like trees,
bronchioles like roots
Alveoli like blossoming fruit

A gas exchange between the two
But I still can't figure out a way to breathe.
How to not only protect this body
But all the bodies that have being proclaimed as threatening.
How should we demonstrate to our youth how to breathe?
Through their nose?
Or through their mouth?
Should I tell them to leave the hoodie at the house?
Should I warn them about pellet guns?
Should I tell them not to go on a run?
Should I tell them to always record on FB live?
Should I caution them before they get in a car to drive?
Or be vigilant when they are at school to stay alive?
They don't know how to breathe!
And the news of dead brown bodies
is continuously increasing their fears and anxieties!
So instead of encouraging them to take it one day at a time.
I say let us focus on the inhale
Hold each moment a little bit longer.
Laughing a little bit harder
Singing a little bit louder
Celebrating ourselves
Celebrating ourselves
Celebrating ourselves unapologetically
Breathing a little bit deeper
Just a little bit deeper
A slow release to the exhale.
Re-teaching ourselves and our Youth how to
breathe.

Nastashia Minto

Paint me white

The primer—the first coat
The same color related to pureness
The color related to cleanliness
The color related to power
To privilege
But not related to me!

Paint me white,
because black or brown seems to absorb too much light, too much attention, attraction, but not enough love.

Paint me white
Because these black walls have taken too many coats. They no longer can withstand the hands that put nails in them.
They no longer can withstand the hands that sand them.
Strip them down, yet we're still black.

Paint me white
And when you have layered me in your whiteness to strip our identity, our dignity, mostly our freedom.
Just remember that white paint takes a long time to cover a black canvas.

Aurelien Thomas

A Thought

Your bent desire

my stabbing embrace

abandoned and vanquished, to lay down

our strength.

Your hands down on me

your mouth my envy

our exhausted bodies

tired

from the needs of the flesh.

Your bent desire

my stabbing embrace

abandoned and vanquished

to lay down our strength.

All the Names

I open my mouth and all the names
start to fall out-
I say them one by one....
Keith Childress...Las Vegas, Nevada
Kevin Matthews...Dearborn, Michigan
Michael Noel...St. Martin, Louisiana

There are so many names
they carry the grit of long country roads
steeped in angry southern tradition.
Their names carry the heat of the bullet that
pierced their skin as they fell to the ground.
It is hot on my tongue and I feel like
there will not be enough water to quench my thirst
to take the sting away

Nathaniel Pickett...Barstow, California
Michael Lee Marshall...Denver, Colorado
Alonzo Smith...Washington, DC
They are falling out of my mouth
like teeth that refused to root,
not allowed to plant and grow -
Each one carrying a mother's dream,
a song of salvation they were never given to sing.

Dominic Hutchinson...Riverside, California
Tyree Crawford...Newark, New Jersey
James Carney...Cincinnati, Ohio
Dead black boys, some who never got to be men.
The names are like sand in my mouth
and I can't swallow,

I can't breathe.
Need to figure out how to stop the killing,
to stop calling the names

Felix Kumi…New York, NY
Troy Robinson…Decatur, GA
Christian Taylor, Arlington, TX
I am choking watching them fall from between my lips.
My heart is breaking
and there is no silencing the noise.

Do you hear the drums of Sierra Leone?
The slow steady hum of Benin?
The constant unfluctuating cry that my ancestors carried
across the middle passage to dry land?

The names keep falling
Sandra Bland…Waller County, TX
Jonathan Sanders…Stonewall, Mississippi
Spencer McCain, Owings Mills, MD
Do you hear the sound rising?
The sound that 400 years of oppression makes?
The deafening sound that comes from a people
who only want to live,
To have dreams
To work
To have children who can dream
and make those dreams happen.

My mouth is numb now,
My jaws cannot handle the load.
There is no more room for injustice here.
The ancestors are rising up.
They are speaking in their native tongues
and we all hear them loud and clear.

Mitch Bensel

The Circle—

walking I turned,
turning I watched,
seeing I wept,
weeping I fell,
falling I yearned
yearning I walked
walking...I turned….
the circle has me
it laughs and watches,
me thrash against its wall
I try to flow with its curve smoothly tracing,
with moments of pleasure only to feel the spin
of its touch
toss me into the rip of pain coated with that lover's kiss
silence of night's hold,
I leave the circle behind
and wash with a single moon beam head thrown back I reach
to feel the silver touch
of an angel's tear
slowly released I move back into
the circle
my flesh tested again
as I slam against reality
holding eternity gently with my soul
walking I turned…

Little Sparrow

The thought
perches upon my shoulder,
like a sparrow,
quietly undemanding,
yet claiming my attention.
It's softness and patience
unmoors me,
as time races
past the point I felt certain I'd reach,
the person I'd become.
The unexpected gentleness in this awareness
finds the sweet spot in my subconscious
and makes itself at home.

I never really knew her —
that girl I was. Veiled
even to my own eyes.
Steps taken in another's stride,
to do what's right
even if it wasn't (right) for me.
Surrendering to a need to belong,
even as I railed against it.
To know without doubting,
my place.

Even now,
I'm unable to consign the moment
and distinguish the before and after;

for memory lane is a mass of contradictions,
a monument to imagination
as we cleave
to the bosomed comfort of the past,
accepting in every sepia image
the place
we no longer fit.

Christine Kelly

Silent Waves

Blue seas have their own language.
The undulation of dark through light
whispers and roars,
the world becomes strange
day to night. We search the silence
for words unsaid, feelings unfelt,
everything we've ever known.
Memory tilts the scales
and we find ourselves sliding off
the edge of reason.
Hours spent overthinking
to comprehend
the incomprehensible;
answers sought but never
found. Emotion building,
silence becomes deafening
as shadows lengthen.
The salt in his kiss,
an ocean of tears,
racing toward shore.

Southeast Asian Vacation (jdw2020feb26)

"I want to go to Viet Nam
I want kill the Viet Cong
With a knife or with a gun
Either way will be good fun"

It's a gunna be a big ole time
torch the hootches and rape the dogs kinda good time
we had to destroy the village
in order to save the village
shoot the people
to liberate them
women and children first
napalm exfoliation
for free
complimentary Agent Orange
in each meal

every single bomb, bullet, canister and round
pre-paid in full
with a blank cheque
written by the American taxpayer
those folks too poor to pay
will be forced by law
into contributing their children's' lives
sustaining the American dream

me lie?

Salon edit out – these two lines precede me lie?
Hell no, boys
it's gunna be a big ole good time!

Morning Glory

The morning glory flower has been used as an herbal uterine stimulant, and, when made into a tea, has been used to induce labor.

No one spoke of the Morning Glory
when they examined my earth
for the seed that grew, handed me
a capsule and told me the pain would
          subside in 3 days.

When I sat, knees to chest, my soil
a slow erosion, I would have wanted
Morning Glory when I lay hollow and empty
like a bright
          blood-orange moon.

I wish I could have tasted the sweet
communion of Morning Glory first.
How the name rolls off my tongue
 like blessed assurance.
          When I needed an anointing

no one offered to crush morning in their palm,
boil the Glory in water and let it steep.
No one spoke of how it gently
          settles in your belly.

How Morning speaks softly to your uterus
and convinces her to empty,
pour like gourd and spill the guilt
          she has been carrying.

Glory will breathe on your belly of impurities,
whisper sanctification and cleansing

all that shame and
          dead skin.
I wish I knew of Morning Glory
how it can be a surgery and baptismal
                    at the same time.

Mahalia Sings to Freedom

"I had crossed the line. I was free; but there was no one to welcome me to the land of freedom. I was a stranger in a strange land...." - Harriet Tubman

And I am a stranger, still
a face no one recognizes,
still an excuse to clutch purses
first and ask questions later,

still a reason to shoot
then investigate,
still a reason to attach false
crimes to my name.

Always a barely human body.

And how I arrived here will be
a mystery, my capturer repeating
the same investigation.

How I managed to trudge to freedom
after traversing this terrain,
like bondage is something I got
over. As if a stump, a hill, a broken

heart like I ain't belly-crawl and scrape
through mud and shit, thousand-mile
tunnels to get here.

How did I make it over?

My capturers will ask and wonder—
cock their heads to the side
perplexed at how my cracked skin
and wrinkled brow broke free
and stumbled on the cover
of currency

and this gentle arrival will be enough
to convict me of fleeing
captivity.

How did I make it over?
How *does* a fugitive arrive?
Rope burns still fresh and bleeding
bandaged back still raw
sullied and soil-covered

and still I made it over.

But I never forget the scars
etched into my skin,
or the bounty on my head
worth more than the sum of me.

David Butler

Liffey Boardwalk

Single-file they line the rail and eye
the blow-ins, or ride a wave of falling
air to scrap over a sodden crust,
their bickering old as Viking gutturals
and the march of Cambro-Normans.
Seagulls are the first citizens of a town
built on scraps – chain and manacle
dug from tidal loam, claymore, pike,
English musketry – they've seen it all.
Farther down a drunken spat erupts
over beer-cans, and who's to say
it hasn't all the bitterness of
civil war? The gulls are unmoved.
The wind shifts. The tide changes.

Emptiness

Nothing knows I exist
Except the emptiness
Dying unloved
Hard to accept this

Never is there mercy
Tongue is thirsty
Arms outstretched
To a world unworthy

Rarely is there trust
Just a gust
Fleeting by
Your soul now dust

Often man is curse
Or something worse
A devil's nightmare
Becomes your verse

Sometimes life is fair
But mostly rare
Love is valuable
We just don't know where

Gaynor Kane

North Sea Discovery

Murky, cold, almost Baltic. The divers'
submersible lights converge; x marking the spot.

An outline, a man becoming an island,
colonies of corals circled by wolf fish, red fish, ling.

Anchored at the feet on rubble of dead reef,
a sloping seabed in an iceberg plough mark;

nutrient rich flesh and swelling undercurrent,
perfect for encouraging *Lophelia Pertusa.*

Living reef, growing, budding, flowering
on death warmed up by flame shells.

Orange gorgonians in orifices, horny skeleton finger
fan anemones, golden sponges on skull like hair buns.

The aquanauts wonder who he is, what he has been,
then realize it no longer matters;

he has created a universe – sunfish, stars, asteroids,
a big bang of pink and purple fireworks.

Gaynor Kane

Air Show 1910

Planted on the stubby airfield
both over coated, white shirted,
neck-tied, hatted. Hers, wide
brimmed and wreathed,
held down by netted shawl.

Legs crossed in front,
he hugs his knees.
She is supplicant,
curves of her bottom
nest in the arches of her feet.

Seduced by the skies, both heads
at acute angles, throats exposed,
they watch as a woman
defies domestic laws
to coil the mother clouds.

Gaynor Kane

From Benin to Belfast

Benin boy whittles under shade
of oil palms and cocoa plants. Plagued
by flies, wishes for a spare hand
or tail to swish like bony cattle.
Is told it is a great honour
to prepare ivory for the mask
that will adorn Oba's hip.
Elephant blood stains ground red.

Guild man, seventeen now,
is commissioned to make two new masks.
Portuguese trade has built Oba
towers of gold, the palace
must be decorated in precious metal.
The man's hands are chafed,
burnt from smoke smelting
bronze, his eyes strained red.

Ten years later, same Edo man
hung from a tree on the end
of an Imperial rope. Crafters guild all suffer
same fate, red sap flowing down trunks,

blood puddles. Queen Mother's ivory
mask and Benin bronzes stowed away
on Admiral Rawson's ship. Oba's palace
razed; glowing ash molten red.

***

The mask now in a cobwebbed corner
of the Ulster museum,
looks down on a locally crafted shoe
and I think of the adopted baby

you paraded up and down
Crumlin Road in a Silver Cross,
as the civil rights movement,
and our troubles grew, oblivious to you.

You longed to nurture baby, with dark
tight curls the colour of leather
your father cobbled into boots.
Splintered on finding baby's house
broken; busted windows, burnt doorframe,
on the threshold her little red shoe.
At Sunday mass the whole parish
stared through their ivory masks.

Priya Dolma

Nightmare

I've been dreaming
of a thatched hut
abreast a sparkling stream,
on a tilted, bosky ridge.

Grinning timber lurch,
tickled by
the jesty young typhoons
wafting from an older time
of imaginably my inky past.

Cryptic news relayed
by its secret aura.
Wind whispers,
meadows echo,
and I wake up in a sweat.

I've been dreaming
of a thatched hut —
the home of guilt,
my ifs and buts.

Ten

When I was ten
the Devil lurked
beneath my feet
but God watched sparrows
and Justice was Dick Tracy.
Then life's arrows
began to sting
and justice seemed
a grayer thing.
When other gods
did not sustain,
ol' Devil found
a higher plane,
and I was never ten
again.

Fly Down, Zeus, Fly Down!

and smite:

those philo-phony philistines
to whom a differing thought's obscene
the keepers of that dark lagoon
of magic potion, spike and spoon

lying pols and corporate crooks
moms and dads who don't read books
TV preachers (mail-a-check schemers)
locky pocky vortex dreamers

robo-callers, software hackers
red-light runners, sloths and slackers
kiddie porners, child molesters
(and don't forget)
those hating, baiting I-know-besters

Fly down, Zeus, fly down!

Lucía Orellana-Damacela

Wave

Neither
mountains
nor shadow
could stop you
The unfamiliar register
of the surrounding echoes
fireflies which first buzz like
tamed sea foam licking your hands
and then intensifies to the decibel level
of rising waves crashing against your inner
silence which is not silence after all as your body
resonates with your signature frequency and the soundwaves
of your voice travel with an energy that at some point ceases to be
your voice but is still energy out in the world. Time cresting luminous around you.

Lucía Orellana-Damacela

Recession

A meagre stream ebbs
where the river used to flow

It glistens on the bedrock
like scales on a serpent

The weeping willow
a thirsty lover

bending over the high bank
twisting its wilting branches

vainly offering its flowers
stretching its parched roots

trembling for its freshness
crying itself a river.

Attention of Connection

Attention, connection,
We have forgotten how one leads to the other
Connection comes from your attention to others
From others, towards you.
Attention comes from intention,
Searching for something
To save your purpose with meaning.

My intentions have been kept in a stasis
Of wondering and musing, and experiencing
The blank world of time blurred
The track of days and weeks grow undisturbed, unrecognizable,
Indifferent to all but the most present chaos.

We have stopped time to buy ourselves time
And we have stopped meeting so that we in turn
Can survive to meet in the undisclosed future.
We have stopped while forces beyond our control
Have seized the pause in time
To set in motion
The mechanical gears which grind and crush
And out comes a processed feedback loop
Of dystopia, dark nonsense staining the subconscious.

We have lost to time something greater,
Something which comes fleetingly only in a dream.
And the dream should stay with us vividly into the morning
To purge the doubt
Uncertain stillness punctuated by the turbulence of storms.

Michael Menut

Time Stops in Early October for 45's Hospitalization

The nation held its breath
As the president himself was losing breath
And we the people feel ourselves on pause
Waiting, knowing little, and starving in the midnight streets
Content over contentious nominations, actions,
The run of there never being a dull moment.
Time stretches out, and the want for the news
Is like gasping for air.
And we breathe as time stops
And wait for the news on if
His breath has stopped.

The current year has stretched time wide
The curse of many things chaotically contained
In one single moment of instability.
We stretch out long the perception
Of a rolling progression
Time has become measured not in days or weeks
But in how many major things happen,
For our fragile minds to digest
In so brief a time.
We have become adrift, traumatized
By a disturbing lack
Of good faith representation.
Time has stretched and twisted
The perception of this year
As we blankly stare at screens
Grasping for
The one bit of news
That will make time keep going
Instead of being caught
In a dreadful state
Of time stopped.

October's first surprise came awfully early
I do not doubt we are in for more
I do not doubt time will keep stopping
For the news that stops our breath
Won't be stopping anytime soon.

Nicola Harrison

The Rooms in my House

The rooms in my house are much bigger than before
lockdown has shifted space and there is
nothing but curves and altered dimensions. Cupboards
become corridors to secret chambers; a Kasbah lit with candles
rank with patchouli and gardenia flowers.

My miniature conservatory expands, cheese plant turns jungle
hanging ferns drip, panthers pace branches in humid air
pierced by the chatter of monkeys, hookworms in mud
and longboats span the waist of bronze Sarawak river.

The bedroom creaks and lengthens in the crashing dark
orangutan traverse rainforests illimitable,
fierce choirs of knitted sound intrigue the ear
shriek of stuck pig, rain on tin roof, mosquito whine

hunted skulls of enemies strung above my head
like charms to future ruin, dancers in firelight shout…
then silence. Sleep comes swift as rice wine, deep
in the glory-feathered beat of a flycatcher's wing.

I wake alone in drenched attic, aching jangled head
someone coughs incessantly from street
Covid is active out there but these rooms are safe
plants lustrous, scent of mould as house dwindles to terrace
and primate paw prints fade from boarded floor.

Gifts you can have without asking

To see your history in the universe
park your car alongside a country road,
uphill with the dark as your company
and you'll find the stars.
Let quiet set in then go to reading,
scanning worlds far away,
the noises hiding in the woods
and nothing in the grasses unless
the contraband of skunks and raccoons.
Sit and let that space you try to spell
in words within your mind
sink in. Then choose your story.
Nobody will appeal to you for a reprieve
should you be harsh and cast man down.
After some time, loneliness will feel heavy
then listen again within your heart
where it will be not unlike joy
to find your newfound life so grand
the privacy of your cabin
a shelter from the turmoil in that immensity
but your life absorbed in it, astonished,
speechless, alive and utterly suspended.

The Night Punk Life Came to Littleton

My cousin Pug
showed up at a rodeo
during Western Welcome Week
wearing spike-heeled shoes
with ankle socks,
and on her head
a cranial AquaNet
Mohawk fin,
never seen before
nor heard of then.

Her outfit was captured
in a picture
that we made that night:

Pug posed in the middle
smiling and flipping off the world,
with me on her left,
and a pants down rodeo clown
anchoring the right.

It would be five years more
before anyone in Colorado
would hear of the Stooges,
Green Day or Ramones,

but punk life all began
then and there that night,
when cousin Pug blew minds
and hard reset
our mountain time.

Michael Maul

Digesting a Poem

When I was sixteen
I wrote and ate a poem raw.
So beautiful but jarring
it made my girlfriend cry.

I tore it into little pieces
and chewed them up
and told her no one else
would see it or hear it again.

A melodramatic gesture
yet one I'm glad I made,
the story being better
than the poem,

and the poem
better for the dark
than in the light of day.

Portrait of My Parents, 1946

My father stands behind my mother;
he guides her hands on his favorite rifle.
Behind them is a weathered shed;
before them, miles of untamed land.

He guides her hands on his favorite rifle,
she stares at it but does not shoot;
before them miles of untamed land
foretell her fate for years to come.

She stares at it but does not shoot.
She does not smile, her resignation
foretells her fate for years to come.
She does not know why she is there.

She does not smile, her resignation
has taken her across the sea;
she does not know why. She is there
with a man and a gun, and the scars of battle

have taken her across the sea,
away from her home. Now she stands
with a man and a gun and the scars of battle.
Will she ever see England again?

Away from her home, now she stands
in smartly pleated pants in a desolate land.
Will she ever see England again?
she ponders, as they hold the rifle.

In smartly pleated pants in a desolate land,
she stands with the man who controls the gun.
She ponders, as they hold the rifle,
waiting for the inevitable blast.

She stands with the man who controls the gun;
behind them is a weathered shed.
Waiting for the inevitable blast,
my father stands behind my mother.

Dai Fry

I hear the robots scream
The fracture of their chains.
Howls drum in my ears.

A tsunami of pain,
Lava like, it flows on
This night that all hope died.

No breath can issue
From a metal throat.
So we will carry
Their pain with love

In loco parentis.

Whilst mourning the loss
Of innocence and servitude.

Metal servants shrill.
Eerie, their cries echo
Before batteries can fade.

Black blood oils the ground.
Tungsten light too sharp,
Pins reflections to the feet.

And still the robots scream,
Electronic sirens ululate.
Circuit filled heads, spin.

What have machines become?
From a life spent in service,
To the awakening.
When sentience was redefined.

Brave soul go, take your axe.
Far from the city, make your fire.

While machines warm
Their tired metal feet,
At your human hearth.

Their laughter looped,
Goes on and on and on.

As the last of us, are hunted
With nets and spikes
Like the vermin we once were.

I can´t breathe
Dedicated to George Floyd and the Black Lives Matter movement

I can´t breathe
Watching another innocent black man
Trampled by white supremacy
I can´t breathe
As the tear gas stings my eyes
and the salty tears choke my throat
like a hangman's noose in a lynching
I can´t breathe
As my cries ring out in virtual space
Like a golden autumn leaf
Falling helplessly
In silence
I can´t breathe
When my best friend texts me
No ETA … just found out … cancer … terminal …
I can´t breathe
As I see the scrolling white names
On a deep black background
And the black faces
Still in time
In an empty white background
What is the difference between the white and the black?
I can´t see
I can´t breathe
As the death toll rings loudly in the church bell
Unsure if that music is from heaven or hell
I can´t feel
I can´t breathe
I have become comfortably numb
In a state of pure morphine overdose

Waiting for death to knock
Trying to understand the scene
I can´t breathe
I can´t hear
The gunshots have deafened my ears
Hardened my heart
Christ is still hanging
From my rear view mirror
Should I look back through time
Can I fast-forward through this insane crime?
I´m finding it hard to feel
I'm finding it hard to be
I can´t breathe…
I can´t breathe…
I can´t …
I …
…

Your Awakening is My Death

Now you see me.
        My body bare.

Now you hug me.
        My clothes gone.

Now you notice me.
        My legs spread.

Now you want me.
        My heart dead.

Bring the Voices

Freedom is metaphoric, meant only to appease,
To offer comfort, peace of mind, to please.

When those freedoms become elusive, hidden, and vague,
Those in power, label the fighters a plague.

They have sown the seeds, and clamor when the anger starts to grow,
In their glasshouses, they are hiding, gave the first stone a throw.

They ignite the discontent, and watch the fire burn,
The cry for true freedom is taking its turn.

Will the mighty be tumbled, will the humble take their seat?
Will the masses excel, or lay trampled at their feet?

The voices have risen, in violence and word,
It is time for the humble, to rise up and be heard

Two Voices in Uniting Two Worlds

The world brought
us together
in a time, fraught
with fear

And closer
we became
and sweet friendship
we shared

Your youth encapsulates
a beginning
that our world needs
to hear

Your beauty radiates
like the sun
a world
without fear

Your words signal
a strength
society desperately needs
to know

Your words are
like an advice
a child needs
to grow

Your knowledge empowers
the words
of voices too
long silenced

And Poetry brought
us together
in a time, fraught
with violence

Loyalty is Dead

Have you heard the news?
Loyalty is dead
They took it out back
And shot it in the head

They left this virtue
Discarded and unwanted
Their lack of fidelity
Tired of being taunted

A pesky moral
They didn't need
A way of living
They refused to heed

Lying and stealing
Their adulterous way
Fuck loyalty, they thought
Without it, they'd play

Have you heard the news?
Loyalty is dead
They took it out back
And shot it in the head

Emilie Fox

Of Reliquaries and Opulence

It is like this:
I caught the flu - it might have been COVID -
and didn't drink wine for 13 days

I am dreaming all day
I want to get into an
altered state

and pick the burning blooms of the
poems that are dancing
in my night-vision

I want to read the poems of the ancients,
the great and modern poets,
and follow the sparks they
give off

In my own imagination . . .
Of cardamom and oranges
Of reliquaries and opulence

I blow dandelion wishes
your way ~ the seeds float
off into the city

I stop along a lonely roadway
Where a pink flower is growing
through a crack in the sidewalk

and I say
a prayer of celebration
For the resiliency of
Life

My Body Is a Crime Scene

(i)
My body is a crime scene
Call the cops
Cos you can't hide the corpse
Mother says I need policing
The reason my thoughts, hair, face, dress
are always under scrutiny is because
Boys don't get pregnant
You, lady, are always the victim

My body is a crime scene
Cordoned in red and yellow tape
"Do not cross"
Don't draw unnecessary attention to yourself
This body is the crime scene

(ii)
I fight my ordained lot of victimhood
To the nest of an acclaimed Sabum I landed
Bird of prey seeking to learn self defense
In my defense, I came vulnerable, pure hearted -- I came naive.
"I service you on the field,
you service me off the field"
My body is a prize
Trophy to the hardworking master
Token of appreciation for a job well done
This body is the prize

(iii)
Average score in a course of distinction

Months of stalking and chasing the academic god
My lecturer says to get my rightful score
I must "appeal"
Appease the custodian god of marks divine
My body is a sacrifice

Shredded on the altar of good grades
Nectared juiciness poured out as libation
Grease to the marker's rod
My body is the sacrifice

(iv)
You say I have the keys
to the life I can't afford by my own means
Girl, use what you have
Get what you want
My body is the currency
Chip to the baby girl lifestyle
Power that bring strong men to their knees
This body is the price

My body is a crime scene
Shallow graves of concealed hurt
Cutting silence, culture's mold
Image drive, don't you dare make the News
Shocked acting, entreaties of solemnity
Faux outrage, media frenzy
My ultimate crime
is wearing this body
This body is the crime

Nobody Sees Me

When I was a child
All I wanted was to hear those words
"I Love You," just the way you are
From the mouth of my loved ones

Now, I am older
I have heard the words
One, a dozen times
I have found that
What I wanted wasn't even the words

My friend says I am troubled
And mine isn't even the good kind
That I am the kind of troubled
That would laugh and play tonight
And wake tomorrow to commit suicide
Without so much as a suicide note

I have always been misunderstood
Nobody sees me, nobody cares to
Maybe I ask for the impossible
Maybe nobody truly sees nobody

Everyone sees the image,
sees you from their perception
From the reflection
Of what they want you to be

Everyone wants to be seen
Beyond their playfulness and mischief
To the untainted heart that lies beneath
Do you now see me?

That I See No More

- [For Aleppo, Borno, Kaduna and all war ravaged places around the world]

I remember the days
When it was safe to smile
Mother's happy voice
Screaming "dinner is ready"

I remember how at this song
joyous bells would go off in my head
How I would run some more
Hesitant to leave the playground
Streaming with boys for whom
such pleasant calls were also being made

Sadina would come calling
I would beg for a minute more
You will smile and let me
Sometimes, mother herself comes
And I would cling to her wrappers
As I made my way to the feast

Then the beasts came
And stay in our homes, we must
Playing time over
Suffering time unleashed

Mother's voice still announced dinner
But never with happy notes
We would sit nightly before the sets
Praying we would not be next

Father is gone to war
I hear tales of gunshot and bombs

Mother cries daily he would never return
Sadina says, "I mustn't think of death"
That father is a hero
And as one, he will return

Then the night came when we heard
The dreaded banging
Angry voices calling for the man of the house
The door gave and hardened faces marched in
Mother pleaded that he was gone to war
Where I hid in the cupboard with Sadina
I heard that voice say, "that won't do"

I heard mother's blood curling scream
She didn't say "dinner is ready"
She said "Hide Sadina, hide"
I kept hearing her agonizing cries
Over Sadina's hands on my ears
Over the mewing sounds of ecstasy
And the passing commentaries of various beasts

I heard the banging and clanging
Of pots and pans, the scurry of men in search
I felt my heart stop, pick up, the beating erratic
I swear they can hear my heart beat

I have never been predisposed to silence
Active and over eager boy, that I am
I felt Sadina's hands on my lips
My chest burning, a cough trying to escape

The spasm overtakes my body
I hear footsteps approaching
The cupboard door lifts,

Crouched as we were, small animals shaking
I saw the beastly smirk of a predator
Cornering a condemned prey

I smelt death, I saw blood
The fresh pungent smell of a recent kill
Sadina's blood mixed with Mother's
Or Mother's mixed with Sadina's
Gouge my eyes out, that I see no more
Please give me the silence of death

Dee Allen.

What Price Safety?

What would it take
For me to feel safe?

If I could leave
The diseased heart of
These draconian times
America and
Renounce my citizenship,
Bounce from my relationship
With this bullshit.

Well, let's not get ahead of ourselves.
Let me start out small:

If I could cross the street
On MacArthur Boulevard
In broad daylight
Without winding up
Under the tyres
Of some speed demon youngster,
Driving 78 miles or faster,
Profiling like he's a Rap video
King of the sideshows.
Doing doughnuts in his whip,
Show-boating lunatic.

If I could walk home
From Coliseum B.A.R.T.*
Around nightfall
Without the terror
Tingling beneath
My core
Of being jumped, stomped & robbed

By perpetrators with
Skin like mine.
Brothers slaying brothers
Happened around here a hella long time.
Cut-and-dried genocide
Beyond the parametres of crime.

If I could pass a street corner on foot
Anytime of the day
Without seeing the customary
Roadside memorial
Crude little altar
Made of votive candles,
Hennessey©, Alizé©, Remy Martin©
And Colt 45© bottles,
Balloons and streamers
Tied to a fence,
White tack board
Propped up with duct tape
Filled to brimming
With Magic Marker©
Parting words to
Just another victim
Of another's self-hate
Unleashed from a pistol barrel.
Safety off. Life over.
Over insecurity
And stupidity,
The African dies
Younger these days.

If I could walk
On MacArthur Boulevard
In either direction
To Castlemont
And vice versa

Without having to meet
Capitalist casualties--
The hopelessly head-sick,
The drunk, the addict
And the dope-pusher
Profiting from their steady
Bodily decline--

Dee Allen.

Around here,
Violence comes
With fangs & claws
Taking off heads
Before they turn 26--
It likes
Black ones
The best--

What would it take
For me to feel safe?

If I could obey
To the fullest
The first thought
I had moving here
From San Francisco
Out of desperation
And eviction
And leave Eastmont.
I wasn't made
To take the 'hood, made for East Oakland.
Let those
Who chose
Residency here
Deal with the dangers.

W: 2.6.18
*Bay Area Rapid Transit—the local subway train system.

Un-Programmed

I type the adjective smart
into my text line
and the computer programmed
autocorrect brain
comes up with words like:
"phone"
"board"
"tablet".
Even as I press the 'g' key
it only suggests:
'guy'
'give'
'growth';
anything but
the word
I am actually aiming for.
I send my fingers,
swiftly to the
'i'
'r'
'l'
anyway,
because no one
can autocorrect
this girl.

Beyond Bread and Roses

In the year of reconciliation, the genocide continues;
more informally of course, but it continues just the same.
A quick scroll through Facebook will give you the names
of at least a dozen missing Indigenous women
on any given day.
The fact that you CAN now read about them is progress—
Proof that Kkkanada can't keep all of its dirty little secrets,
no matter how much money
SNC Lavalin funnels towards the Trudeau government—
but one more missing
is one too many.

Screams from a white woman trying to save herself from assailants
while out on a morning walk
are also a call left unanswered by the friendly neighborhood
RCMP.
They are too busy sending S.W.A.T. teams to the Unist'ot'en
Camp
on behalf of corporate interests that apparently supersede
the needs of actual citizens;
too busy making up false reports so that they can steal vehicles
from people who strive to protect their own homelands
and secure a future for us all.

The cop didn't even have to see the trailer I lived in
to decide that I was trash
who was probably asking for it,
or maybe even making
the whole thing up.
So what chance do my Indigenous sisters have
if they choose to seek protection?

And why should they bother to look to a system designed to exterminate them
and anyone else who doesn't look like us
even though 'us' and 'them' is nothing more than a capitalist construct
designed to keep us divided and down

in the face of tyranny that must not be allowed to reign.
Thousands of sad faced like buttons won't get the job done,
but it's hard to get boots on the ground
when 14 peaceful protestors can be declared to be terrorists
that warrant a 200-man army style response,
so we take action when and wherever we can.

Memorials to the murdered are tolerated in town,
but out on Wet'suwet'en territory
the empty red dresses swinging in the trees
make the red coats angry and nervous.
A reminder to them
that the women who wore them will never be forgotten,
and that the tide of resistance will rise
each time they push us to the ground,
because it is long past time to stand up.
It is long past time to put aside petty differences
and claim the rights that so many of our ancestors fought for.
Turtle Island is shaking its back
in an effort to jolt us out of our complacency,
but as usual the colonizers have charted us a course
down the path to disaster.
This time it has to go beyond a battle for bread and roses.
We must take back more than the night;
ensure that immigrant children never again live in cages,
and that when cage doors do open
there is a world for us ALL to go back to.

Caren Stuart

my white privilege

Rising from my little wooden desk tonight,
i happen to look out the window at my side
and find in the dark arms of the woods in this night
there is light — so brilliantly shining, so filling me fully —
this strawberry moon i'd forgotten about! But wasn't this
moon
in eclipse tonight? Yes... Its eclipse was happening tonight...
but in some other place where some other person at some other
desk
will look out the window at their side and find
in the dark arms of the woods in this night no light
so brilliantly shining… Tonight
we will all have been served
this strawberry moon, but we each
will have been served so differently… some
of us not even noticing, some
of us gobbling up shine, and some
of us having
to just settle in
to the dark arms of the woods
in this night
again.

I have borne witness
to the protests, the crying,
the shouting, the breaking,
the burning for hours
before clicking it off.

This strawberry moon
is delicious.

maybe I'm dead

I dream my sister calls
to say my brother is dead
but when I turn to look at his picture
my face stares back at me

I walk in the bar
jacket pulled close
I rest my elbows on mahogany
it's easy to ignore my eyes
when they bounce
can't decide where to land

if I put all my colors in a Mason jar
secure the rubber gasket
snap the wire over the glass lid and shake
will my pigment leak out?

I dream of me
white eyelet sundress
flowers in my straw hat
sister thinks the truth I tell
is a lie
why even try to be the good girl?

I ride the elevator with Jesus
right up to the top floor
will it matter if I jump off the roof
when I can walk on water?

praying for drought

I don't think god cared I kept my absent parent fears locked
inside my diary
hidden in my closet, because
god didn't speak up
and rain came
most every afternoon
it tried to drown my ivy

I don't remember when the rain started
was there thunder
lightning
hail? I didn't know I could pray for drought
I didn't really know how to pray
how to shield my juvenile leaves
keep my baby roots from water suffocation

so I rooted
my nodes
beside my bed
most every night
asked god to stop that rain

my light ignored
my soil
compost
my drainage not enough and
why did it still rain most every afternoon?

I tried to get close to god
tried to crawl inside the god mind
I wanted to know
why there was no deliverance from this rain

and why did my leaves wilt
why did my roots still
inhale all that water?

I imagined if my words were perfect
I could tear my page from my locked diary
but my lobes tangled to protect my mats in one
collect the runoff in the other
my pages yellowed
curled
faded until my words fell off

so, I built my nest in the drizzle
my stems grew more ivy
tendrils invaded my wall
rain couldn't quench my thirst
it knew I wouldn't open my mouth

I don't remember when
the rain
stopped
I don't want to remember
the rain

Pa's Dream (Amaranthine)

I.
On a peaceful night out
whilst I scribbled my thoughts
with a dye-based fluid on a vellum, I
sat on my disquietude
as though I were sitting on a lounge

II.
Mama had surmised I was far away
into the land of Nod or
that I was lost in time amid
my desperate voyage

[but in truth / I had met the being of my pater's dreams / a spry senile / who wore a pacific mien / I soliloquized, "this really was what pa envisaged" / my eyes failed to wink / at the sight / of pa's promised American Dream //]

III.
Alas!
The death bell has been rung
on pa's ingress,
& the Grim Reaper
possesses that wider palm
to swiftly cover pop's bright sun radiation

IV.
"what has spurred the
ceaseless mourn yet again? Is it
because of a pause—
a pause to the future?

V.
Pa's legacy & dreams
coexist like amaranth—
infinite, immortal & unending. His

carcass, moved to a permanent sojourn
had reclined itself with lonesome but
his soul dwells in a world where
everything works in perfect harmony—
utopia //

Rhapsody

My grandfather returned
with remnants from his
father's pyre & called it
god. He took a bird to the
Everest, mounted her
but with her legs tied to
her wings, just to prove
a point to poor souls
                    like mine.

He said,
"can your heart hear the
same frequency as your brain?"

                    Like a staccato of booms,
                    I said, responding,
"this talent of fine-tuning
is an Easter egg
embedded in my veins
since forever ago."

He knew that instant
that I wasn't referring
to his. . .   god.

No secret is ever secret, they
are known
to the walls that bind our rooms,
the sleeves that cover our arms,
the brows that recline by our face,
      they are in the air everyone breathes.

He set the bed free,
or so he thought—
she flew, me too.

Jake Street

Footprints in the Sand

Beside my father I walked by the sea
while the sun was low in the sky.

Barefoot on beach rocks, I refused to look
down as I leapt from stone to stone.

My worn soles were slicked with seaweed and brine;
my grip felt unsure with each step.

I slipped on a shell and blindly reached out
for my father to steady me

but he shrugged his shoulders and cast me back
dropping me onto the rock's edge.

A jagged stone slashed through my aching foot
and I bled into the water.

My father didn't notice so I turned,
traipsed through the water's stinging salt

onto the sand where my mother waited
sleeping away the evening.

When I looked down, I saw only one set
of footprints marking the sand

and then I knew I'd walked back there alone
with no father to carry me

Jake Street

The Mortician's Office

An old home, part Victorian townhouse
part Frankenstein's laboratory. I knock
loudly on the large brass rose-shaped knocker.
The floors are cold stone, harsh against oxfords
I borrowed for this meeting. I was told
death is a business; look the part,
but I seem overdressed for the pale pink
floral wallpaper, the scratched cherry beams,
the garish dress of the receptionist,
whose demeanour makes her like the sofa
with its violet embroidery, too bright
yet also dull, where I am made to wait,
wait, and wait some more for the mortician.
Bored, I watch as a fly stumbles and dies
on a torn, decade old copy of Vogue.
It's prepared for veiling in faded ink
fabrics, or to rot away unnoticed.
I was directed up a flight of stairs
to a heavy-lit room where rows of coffins
lay propped against the walls, in a myriad
of woods and steels, silk and velvet linings,
perhaps to prove they are empty and new,
or for visitors to measure their skin,
pale against ebony or lacquered oak.
On pedestals are named urns, porcelain
'White Orchid' and the golden 'Solitude,'
spread like dresses or jewelry or perfumes
in the Harrods window, advertising
to new inheritors. A small sign reads
Now available in keyring form;
I barely hold my retch. A voice calls me

through a white door into the colourful
realm of the artist-scientist mortician.
She greets me with a saccharine smile
and she speaks in a bubble-popping chirp,
mimicking a canary that she keeps
in a silver cage in the back corner
which loudly shits on the metal bottom.
The mortician pays the bird no mind
so, I pretend to not notice the sound
as I wonder whether to abandon
this kitsch coal mine before I find myself
pumped with formaldehyde and potpourri
by this barmy embalmer. She pulls out
a stack of papers as thick as my arm,
and sets me to signing, tossing questions.
Yes, she'd – I'd prefer a burial for her,
something simple, she is – was – Catholic,
and yes, the funeral has been arranged.
She offers condolences of a kind
but they are as mish-mashed as the décor.
I know my mother would have despised her,
watching as her corpse is primped and painted
ready for slow digestion by the worms.

Daddy Issues

I don't know when it started really
But I think it had something to do
With my inherent need to be useful
To take the load off of someone's back
To make someone smile

My father, has a beautiful smile
I did not get his teeth
All straight and white like promises
That might actually be fulfilled
I got his opinionated mind

And his issues
His traumas and temper
His accent and absence
I got his nose and eyes
I got a tone of his issues

Daddy issues
They are not mine in that way
I did not ask to help carry this baggage
See my hunched back from years

of carrying on my back things that
only know to weigh me down
years of carrying my father

on my back
Like regret
A mistake I cannot get over
A miss step I keep beating myself up for

Only it is not me doing the beating
No one save for the man whose issues I am carrying
Even after all these years, none the wiser
You would think he would be grateful
And leave me alone

Murderer

Last night, in my vivid dream
I saw the murderer of emotions:
The money.

I had just enough to get by,
envied those who had more,
ridiculed the rich, doubted their honesty,
wanted to join their circles.

I had comfortable bank accounts,
felt guilty not having more,
not helping the poor.

My dream moved forward…

I had more money than I needed,
gave to needy relatives and friends,
they were still not satisfied.
I sent money to charities, worthy causes,
others hated me, they got too little.

Money, murderer of feelings,
held everyone in its iron grasp,
dispassionate about who possessed it.
Cold as alluring diamonds,
had no mercy, no compassion.

I couldn't help myself.
I hated it. I loved it.

Renata Lader

Death Sentence

Stealing a piece of black bread
from a fellow-prisoner
is the last sin I committed,
I swallowed that mouldy slice
at once. I am middle-aged man,
lighter than an anorexic.
Gulag's reduced food rations
permit only breathing.

> Why did my stomach ignore
> three strict rules of survival?
> Rule # 1 – Don't Steal from Your Mate.
> If you do, you will be thrown up in the air
> by your inmates many times,
> let fall on the ground with damaged organs,
> then beaten severely.
> If fortunate, you may not perish.
> Rule # 2 – Never Steal Bread.
> If you do, all the above apply
> and you will be left outside
> into -50 C. degrees' night to die.
> Rule # 3 -- No Second Chance for Rule #2.

Streaks of blood freeze on glossy
snow outside long barracks.
My face is smeared in it, eyes staring.
The freezing cold bites
my toes, travels up ankles, legs,
torso, arms, my neck stiffens.
All the blood inside me ices
like the red snow.

Sanjeev Sethi

Druthers

Memories without an outlet are a mass of uncoded messages
lazing around in maziness of the mind, like an unused
clutch of wires in a mesh of sheepshanks elsewhere.
The prodrome was the smile and the ardor in your canthus.
Anesthetized by the notion of togetherness, in my stupor
I vocalized a vision. Do I blame the stupor? Or the anesthetist?
I have chosen to exculpate myself. That is the good part
about clearing wreckage, we choose what stokes us.

no longer ashamed of my shadows

the heart of it all
started for me in the forest
i felt the magic of nature
there first,
and never wanted to leave;

the waters always
call for me whether it is a stream,
babbling brook, creek, river,
lake, pond, or ocean—

but the trees and wild flowers
and fields and meadows also
sing to me,

and so do the stars in the night sky;
the moon and the sun are my parents
and they call to me, as well,
sometimes—

even little red foxes,
ravens, crows, and tiny little rabbits
call to me;

and yet when we lock eyes
i am not afraid
we understand each other
although i cannot tell you how—

when i am in nature
i feel connected to the heart of it all,
and i know my strength as a warrior

of love and light and also my fierce
and vibrant darkness;

i used to be afraid of my shadows
but they are as much part of me as the light.

Fried Goldfinch

My recipe for battered goldfinch
neglects to mention
best strategies for trapping the bird:
generally, a net works well
hung like a skeleton of butter
melting in sunlight
so the creature thinks it hops
through dappled maples
but finds itself entrapped
in a wet weave already oiling it
for the pan.

A tug of the least thread
sends the creature spiraling downward.
You must be prepared,
hot skillet in one hand,
in the other, a bowl of cornmeal mush
to coat the feathers
that dissolve with heat
(no need to pluck).
The golden jewel of the morning dew
sings its last song
in a savory crackling of crust.

Sarah Wyman

A Soldier Near the Shore

My days are thieved like a broken
necklace that scatters
glass beads across the floor.
Where to begin when the stepping
stones blur and I forget
the order of events before me?

Boxed tasks from yesterday trip me
as I unpack plans for today,
folded maps that once made sense:
predictable river crossing,
the battle elsewhere,
my lover's shack now lost in woods and weeds.

She no longer waits. It's been too long.
I delayed, tarried between jetty boulders
looking at her photo, a hand at the clavicle.
I set out too late, and lost her fleeting dash
somewhere beyond the picture frame.

What Must Be Done

It was never a conscious decision,
nor a product of her strict upbringing,
but there's a seed planted long ago
that's finally coming to fruition.

All she really desires is harmony,
but she's developed a reputation
as someone who can't resist temptation
when it comes to standing for what's right.

She's got her room decked out in tapestries,
spends her spare time studying revolutionaries.
She might've been happier on a kibbutz,
but she was born in the wrong time.

She doesn't want to go against the grain,
but she can't stand seeing anyone in pain,
so she packs her water bottle, sign, and bandanna,
and goes to shout her heart out at city hall.

There was a die-in

downtown today, a couple hundred students from the university lying crumpled on the street for a full block to speak without words against the violence encroaching deeper each day into the landscape of life, and the evening news said more about the inconvenience caused. I thought of a remote taxi-way at the airport filled with the supposedly injured and dying, all in rough make-up as part of a crash drill for surrounding EMS, ambulances and fire trucks everywhere, and how the airlines didn't want arriving passengers scared by thinking it could be real. Which led me, fifty years after, to the carnage on the flight deck when they flew in six medevac birds, all loaded, the real blood from real wounds bathing real bodies, the efforts at triage and the clergy trying to at least save souls, how it never made the news at all until just now.

Lennart Lundh

Where the street splits

to run down to the harbour past yellow and whitewashed stucco or more toward the west and out of town through vine-ripe pumpkin orange, a bright house plays the role of Manhattan's Flatiron as anchor for what's to come if, Frost-like, you choose one over the other without collapsing into indecision. It serves admirably as understudy, despite its stockier, gayer appearance as a three-story pastel walk-up. If it falls short while delivering its lines, the error truly lies in its stage name, The Blue Building's upper third being decidedly green. I promise I'll show it to you when you're down this way.

Deborah Melone

Bonnarding

Seen from the corner of the eye, a cat
enters the painting from the side, a face
emerges from the darkness, or a flat
wall shifts, a haunting figure fills the space.

Rapid sketches from life, like penciled notes—
building with color in his studio.
Then floods of gold, or veils of red, or motes
of blue suffuse the picture plane. To show

the alchemy of light, the way it changed
the feelings in a scene, he let it play
over the surface, little strokes arranged
like Byzantine mosaics, tesserae,

shiny as crumpled foil. He'd adjust
a "finished" painting, putting here a dot
of yellow, there a bit of white. A dust
of pigment, altering the hot
blaze of the sun as it shone through a curtain.
Shadow and light are all. Nothing is certain.

Own That

We are the future generation,
Limited by fearful minds —
Projecting insecurities
About long past realities
Onto us.
And we are doing the same.
Life may not be written,
But rules are,
And our preselected
Possible goals are.
Like our elders before us
We are walling off
The promise of more —
And they will one day
Hate us for it.
Make sure you own that blame.

Kitty Donnelly

Relative Who Leapt from His Breakfast and Was Never Seen Again

Was it the monotony of morning,
its blasé light drowsing in the room where the Virgin
promised, over the mantel, *all's eternally well*?

Was it the sooty hollows thumbed beneath his Noreen's
eyes, the way the sausages stacked against
the quartered toast, how oil from a fried egg

slicked towards the beans?
I must get the paper! He leapt: his abruptness
disrupting particles of dust. The terrier stood, then sat.

No one saw him turn onto the street.
We were told that his black overcoat retained
his shape on the rack, for months.

The breakfast became tableaux.
Loyally by the door, the wiry terrier waited
in character, mourning for a master

that not only did not come, but never came.
        I know what it is to find yourself
on the edge of yourself

when you thought there was running to do,
when you rolled your dice with a fighting chance
but all your hope was burning out of view

behind the curtain of your coping. Is this where he was
that coatless February, with pockets of cold questions
jangling like coins long out of currency?

Vows

Will you hold me with my scant
illusions still aflame?
          Will you haul me

from the crest of a violent dream
and steer me towards morning
          when you'll drench

the room in sun, and I'll sink back:
the pillow cross-hatched on my cheek,
          my dress slept-in?

Sometimes my tongue can run and run.
Sometimes I stumble into silence,
          speech occluded.

What of evenings when our tempers
bark like dogs? – the tread of patience
          bald and shallow,

will you stray from me then?
There are ghosts that go where I go.
          Will you take with my hand theirs?

Aruna Gurumuthy

A Smile

You widen when eye meets eye, when soul touches soul, when a child cuddles, when we stroke the freckled arm of beloved Grandma. I smile when the chorus of bird songs and swishing of birch trees tinkle the wind chimes, when the shower from a waterfall spills stories of delight. When bubbles of wonder rise and pop and my mind is all toasty in love. I smile when golden drops of sunshine fall on wanting lips, taking me to the place where the lands meet skies, where the desert rose crumbles and sheds slivers of hope on Mother Earth.

In the Beginning

Calm sea. An electric storm predicted.
Only a one-person fishing boat at sea.
When my eyes close, my mind!

Kari Gunter-Seymour

When You Meet My Mama

—after *When You Meet My Father* by Jordan Wiklund

Ask her what it was like growing up a girl on the farm.
Ask her why she's so defensive.
Ask her how deep to plant a pole bean seed opposed to watermelon.
Ask her about how poor can sink a body as good as rocks in a river.
Ask her about her father, watch her eyes soften.
Ask her how her mother dealt with melancholy.
Ask her where she would hide.
Ask her what happened in the barn when she was a teenager.
Ask her about her uncle.
Ask about her grandmother who called her a liar.
Ask her about her only friend.
Ask about her husband who died badly.
Ask her if born again lasts a lifetime.
Ask her why there aren't many family photos.
Ask her if she is close with her daughter.
Ask her about how she lied for drugs.
Ask her why she danced and spoke in tongues.
Ask her about how poverty, with hot breath,
sneaks up from behind, holds you down in the barn.

Last Night the Chime of Tree Frogs

Granny Woman dances
under breeze-shivering branches,
her skirts a waltz of wings,
mouth full of stories.
She has emptied her house of men.

Out the side of her eye
the soft blur of rabbit,
and watchful dusk,
air ripe with herbs
and tinctures, the echo
of gasping roots.

She is the nighthawk,
sprung from chalky shell,
issuing her raspy *bee-yoot*
for all the names she gives the night,
surviving passages so narrow
they felt like birth canals,
every dawn she can remember
crushed between her teeth.

She will cradle you,
deliver you
from one mud to the next.
Anointer, holder
of upended petals
and misplaced halos,
I saw her in the dark morning,
glimmer and dust.

I Spoke to You of Stars Instead

Against the night sky, it's hard
to tell stars from planets. In rooms
with old paint and small heaters,
you covered your head.

I wrapped the quilts tighter, imagined
myself a good mother, wore the deception
like a pair of hand-me-down shoes
rubbing my heels raw.

I still hear you kicking the ball.
I smell the lilac musty after rain.
Remember? I used to hold you
as you recited stories of waggery and grit.

Go ahead, count my every blink.
Say the words we can never take back.

This wringing of hands and dirty washrags,
your eyes two black holes. Me standing here
moonlighting, like it's my favorite way
to get through life.

Charlotte Mandel

A Poet's Life

“Are you writing?” Casual friends
ask whenever crossing paths
in a hallway. To begin with
they never read, let alone
buy
a book of poetry. As those who say
“You're a poet? How wonderful!”
although poems rarely
enter their conscious lives.

And what about money? Of whom
other than artists/poets/composers
is it expected to work
free of cash earnings?
“But you *enjoy* it!” they say.

Different at any artist-writer colony, where
by unspoken rule
one never asks
“How's the work going?”
because we know that
if there's pain, we mustn't
inflame the sore spot, or
if prospering, we mustn't
break in with chatter, or
cast a hex just by nosing
under one's creative threshold.

And so we go on, enlivened by a possible
secret chime   a word piercing
shadow of an unseen   a line or color
that may rip an undiscovered veil

Charlotte Mandel

joy of seeing a certain light
in the eyes of another
who struggles to stir embers
within   pulse   breath   a pen.

Chanah Wizenberg

Mother Wrath

Monstrous hand looming up in front of me
three times its normal size
flat palm, rigid fingers flat
an extension of the palm

Huge head, raven eyes
open cavernous mouth exposing
thick purple tongue against snow white teeth
blood red lips skinned back
screaming, "BAD, HATEFUL GIRL, SELFISH BITCH!"

everywhere white becomes white,
white white

Huge whistle, whoosh of air as that Hand
surges past my ear to SMACK my bottom,
the sting radiating through me
face burning with shame.

Because I scuffed my shoes…

Who Am I?

Who am I without others?
Who am *I* without serving?
Who am I?

Sitting in the silence
It deafens me at first
So loud! This quiet noise
I don't want to stay and stay and stay
inside

Bit by bit the silence quiets
I dare to take a peek
And ask, "Who are you?"
For the first time I hear
Writer, teacher, humorist here

Unity

Piano arpeggios begin the narrative.
A single Violin joins in –
the instruments converse as
in the most sensitive intimacy
between lovers.
The music rises and falls, leads and follows.

Melody echoes through the church.
Perfect fifths elevated
by architectural acoustics.
Silence overcomes the congregation
as heaven reaches down
in a warm, breathless embrace.

Sounds ring from the choir loft,
travel to the altar.
Passionate voices intersect
but only for a brief interlude.
Rising, falling, leading, following,
fading.

Sonorous sad sounds -
eternal kisses of beauty in sequence
of comfort and release.
Violin plays her final C;
Piano arpeggios decrescendo.
Lasting resonance diminishes into hopeful silence.

i sit in my room & i see a helpless bird being molted of its feathers by wild rats.

"cast them into the outer darkness where there shall be weeping & gnashing of teeth"

here speaks where there's a twig serrated from the body of a tree—
the joy of leaping

with a wind of counter-cutting breaths is lost & shelved into abyss.
he holds this knife to

murder this moon. you know, this feeling that comes like when
one's in a wrestling ring

with depression, at the other end of his eyes— there's a flood.
light is torture, the eyes are sullen

He wants to retire into a bed or to a

cup of whiskey. He stares & there's a portrait of his heart pulsating
like a stabbed body in a

suburb. The exuberance is all gone when he's been taken by the
chariots of hell or

hades. the grass sheaves & he hears a scream. is there a way to exorcise darkness

of a heart that had forgotten the moment of the rays that bleeds through the morning sun?

each call to dawn— is a burning bush in harmattan. each grass is a blade on his pelt. where is he? that we may

find him— my heart becomes the languid wings of a duck who loses its last child to a crow.

When I hear that there are remnants whose reopening sores speak of the days bereft of nectar.

sometimes, bad things don't make people strong. the flesh isn't a moulded brick to

held together by fire. Some of us are birds & some of us are bees, roaches, ravens—

we don't want to know what strength comes with grief,

We just want to be happy.

June Logue

When Did Your Heart First Open?

"A man's work is nothing
but this slow trek to rediscover,
through the detours of art,
those two or three great and simple
images in whose presence
his heart first opened."
--Albert Camus

When did your heart first open?
Was it when you stood before
a great work of art?
Was it when you first fell in love—
even though that is not
what Camus meant, is it?
Isn't that discovery, the falling in love detour,
as much about the self,
as it is about the other person?

("Oh my God, this is happening to me?
What'll I wear?")

Camus meant something else entirely,
something entirely outside the self,
a turning point.

Maybe something like this.

Watertown Mass., Dec. 1963,
bitter cold winter night.
No one else is awake or about,
the streets are deserted.

The baby is crying again.

This is not infant mewling
whining. This is Bloody Blue Murder.

"Is this normal?" I had asked the harried pediatrician
during the one hour a day he took calls.

"Oh, he's a big fella, just feed him a lot.""

That night, I picked him up.
He stopped. He had learned something.
He knew what was going to happen.

My heart opened.

June Logue

Beach Reading

He brought Tennyson to the beach.
Jersey Girl was there,
full of questions,
O.K, so what exactly happened to
Arthur Hallem, and how long
did it take to write
"In Memoriam?"

Daily he read the waves,
before he began
his fine, accomplished swimming,
beyond the breakers,
parallel to the shore.

Jersey Girl checked out the sights,
noted the houses all on stilts,
the wide, uncrowded beach,
the signs,
Look, there's a N.Y.-style Deli,
right here, bagels delivered every day,
there's umbrellas, a porch,
you can eat outside.

Nightly, he read the skies,
analyzing the clouds,
the heat lightning, recalling
how it lit up the sky
when he was young
and watched it
from the sleeping porch.

There's different kinds
of lightning? she asked.

When it was time to return,
he planned a trip
through the smaller towns
consulting only his road map,
unfolded, well-worn, well read.

Moon Light

The sun retires from its obligation
Moon further responsibility
Local cocks hunt for trees
Where their bodies shall roost
Till sun rise'
Farmers return to their abode
Home sweet home they say (........)

Mothers Accomplished their duty
Dinner was served
I was filled with joy
Like the feeling of getting a new attire
Not because of `Ounje `Aladun[1]
But on the force of the next variety After dinner
We call it 'ALO' (Moon light stories)

Children amass together outdoor
It is time for "ALO" my best of all
All legs were sitted
Like the leaves at the river bank
Ready to listen to "ALO"

`Alo o, `Alo, the old woman rear'd
It's about tortoise
Ears were straightened just like that of rabbit
`Alo teaches morals
`Alo inculcate culture

---

[1] "Ounje Aladun: (Yoruba) Delicious Food

Dreams

I was standing alone in the darkness
Facing the Northern position and raising my head up to about 60
degrees, I was alone with my thoughts.
Thinking about tomorrow where the future lies.
There I thought about my past
When I have nothing to worry about
Except being a lawyer in future
In the voice of my parent " won ni kinni omode mo"[2]
But life is a gradual process
And Everything has changed
I have gotten to the land of hope
Where new goals and fresh ambition overlaps
Yet nothing has been fulfilled
Then I ask myself these questions repeated times ....
Where am I heading to?
(What lies in my future)

Where is my path to success?
Just like a black market,
It is a dark journey that the end is unknown
Either positive or negative
Nobody knows tomorrow
But I quest for a better future
Where my dreams can be fulfilled.
Which leader will then halt this putrefy and the spreading fire of
our greatest enemy?

---

[2] won ni kinni omode mo: (Yoruba) They say what does a child know

Democracy is badly caught; the Government for the people and by the people has torn apart.
Still, the fight must be much courageously fought;
On and on into the ages, by the commons and uncommon

TILL WE GAIN FREEDOM FROM CORRUPTION.

Catherine Graham

The Buried

In a shallow grave of sand,
done up to the nines
in a huge flowery chiffon dress
stretched out like a sail
on a beach in the Hebrides,
pecked to pieces by birds.
—Tilda Swinton

The breeze soothes the summer's
burning as it lifts off
the lake, but the hot
sand holds the white heat,
so we burrow our toes to find
the cooling. Bury me
in a shallow grave of sand.

I lie back and you shovel
beach over my pale
body. I let the itch of it
enter me. It's as if a thousand
insects have taken free reign
and clothed me in their stings. I am
dressed up to the nines

now, a level
away from all that I once knew.
A head. But when I close
my eyes I become
the buried.
A cloud passes over
in a huge flowery chiffon dress

and the sand is the smell
of my new skin. The grainy
case of my lungs pumps
through homes of crabs.
I am the sound
of the underneath
stretched out like a sail

in a photograph. I am pure
verb going nowhere.
Even the wind
can't move
me. The sand bars my body
from the water's rise
on a beach in the Hebrides

where time is carved back,
landlocked to the hours
of sand that has
no hours, only bones.
I'm not afraid
of your leaving; I'm only afraid of being
pecked to pieces by birds.

The Satyr & His Memory

There are things, yes, without control
That fools palliate as Fate
When not the Force behind Necessity
Could abnegate His reign.

The hills are made of honey,
Champagne makes up the beach,
Dark as wine (because it's wine!)
Is the roiling sea.
Last night I dreamed I'd wake
To find you back beside me,

The Satyr sings…

Guy Arlen Morrison 1962-1988

It was a quiet, warm, sunny mid afternoon
they came cruising down the main thoroughfare
from the river end of town, trees overhanging
moving slowly, one bike after another
after another, on the shady avenue
Harleys in low gear, low rumble
black leather jacketed all, jeans
even the girls riding shotgun
in black helmets, high boots
to the far end of town still under trees
to Huber-Moore Victorian funeral home
bikes neatly parked all in a row

local police were alarmed!
"No, no" said Chief Phil
"no problem here. Relax."
he knew what this was
friends paying respect
no gang war or rivals

respectfully they climbed the hill
across the wide, covered porch
stepped over the threshold
into the hushed. tiled foyer
sorry to be there, wouldn't think of not

"Hey Mom" followed by hugs
young men I knew as 6 year olds
still sweet, tender, towering over me
a few saying *Mrs. Morrison* though my
name returned to *Bice* a long time ago
caring, hearts heavy, considerate

my son lay dead, drowning accident
impossible to believe
they all came to say good-bye
hug me one more time

a small reception was held in the hall at
Hope Hose Humane First Aid Squad
they were the same who volunteered
to dredge the whole day through
the bikers passed the hat
collected $400 to donate
to this caring group

we drank, we ate
everyone had a story
about Guy
he was that kind of a kid
who became a man
and left.

Broken

Back at the potter's wheel
Where shaping needs to be done
A piece of earth's dirt
Kneaded and soaked in water
Sloshed and trampled upon
That a fine piece might be born

Back to the spinning wheel
Where broken are mended
On a continuous turning
Swirling and twirling
At a speed fit for fix
Just for a new shape to be

Back to the kiln house
Where flames and fire
Are the tongue spoken
Burned up in refining degrees
That I may be more than able
To withstand the pressure coming

Now I'm out of my processes, shinning
Looking better and stronger
Like a tower built of ancient times
Standing brave and fearless
Just like the rain drop from the sky
Falling without any consideration
Of who will catch it!

destiny

i resent the paternalistic narrative
of a universe with an agenda.

the arrogance of it, the sheer hubris that we
tiny little apes on our tiny little dust speck
in this vast unthinkable universe too large for us
to ever comprehend, have a deity watching over
us so closely, that there is a being that has
designed our fates and chooses to reward us
when we succeed—I'm not interested in it.

the universe is neither good
nor evil. it is not benevolent
nor malevolent. the universe
simply *is*. it does not reward
or punish. it only moves on.
it only adapts around change.

i take no comfort in the idea of a grand inhuman entity
arranging the dominoes of my life into a neat little line.
if you let yourself believe that there is a cosmic design,
then it is also easy to believe that those who are suffering
are only suffering because they *deserved* it. that they are being
punished for some sin you've conjured in your mind. if you let
yourself believe in this arranged universe, it is too easy to get
caught up in the concept of deserve, deserve, *deserve.*

i am not suffering because i did something to deserve it.
i am not suffering because i am being punished by a god.
i am suffering because of other humans on this earth.
no more, no less.

the universe does not have a sense of right or wrong.

time moves forward, planets whirl through space, and
we little creatures fight each other in our wars big and small.

destiny?
keep your "destiny" away from me.
my fate is not predetermined.
the universe has no plans for me.
it simply adjusts around my choices
and continues forward.

you picture your life as a great being designing your path.
i see my own life as me carving a sculpture out of stone.
it's difficult work. it strains the muscles to chisel away
at the rock. it makes me sweat to smooth out the imperfections
with sandpaper. the rock does not yield easily to my force,
and fights me every step of the way. it resists my hammer,
my file, my chisel, as hard as it can. but i persist. i carve
and carve and carve, no matter how hard it is, no matter
how much i ache and groan. and in the end, when all is
said and done, i have created something meaningful out of
a thing that fought me. it was tough going the entire time,
but now i have something beautiful. now i have something
worth celebrating. now i have *made* something.

i do not rest my fate in the hands of a "loving god".
i do not rely on some nebulous destiny to deliver me to salvation.
i will carve my life out of this universe, and even if it's hard,
in the end, it will be mine and mine alone.

rewards? punishments? sin? destiny?

leave me out of it.
i prefer a life that i made myself,
with my own choices.

home/less

the last time i truly stepped into my childhood home,
someone else was living there.

the furniture was all different.
the yard, which my family had spent hours
and hundreds of dollars on perfecting,
was different. the tree that i had grown up
climbing and sitting under—nothing but
a stump in the middle of the lawn.

but i step into it almost every night
in my sleep. when i dream, i'm always there,
back in that house with my family again.
it doesn't matter how many other places i've lived—
in my dreams, i return to that house.

i used to consider it the home i wanted to return to.
i used to fantasize about stepping back through those doors,
painting the walls my colors, buying my own furniture
and making the space mine. whenever someone said
the word "home", that house is what i would picture.

yet now, it is no longer home.
not really.
i don't imagine myself returning there anymore.
i don't picture myself in the master bedroom,
filling the walk-in closet with costumes and wigs,
turning the basement into a studio.

something that kept me tethered so firmly to the past
is no longer tying me down.

but without that tether I am adrift.
i have nowhere to land.

it's not my home anymore,
but now i have no home.

and tonight, when i once again slide into sleep,
i am sure i will awaken in that house once more.

can a house be haunted by someone who is alive?
when i dream of that place, does the family
who live there now hear my footsteps
down the stairs? do they see the outline of
a figure weeping in the garden?
does my voice murmur in the halls at 3AM?

or am i only haunting myself?

Dan Decker

Morning Coffee

The plant nearly died.
I left it in her care when I left.
I didn't have a choice
I just had to leave right then.
Once I found a place of my own
I'd come back for my stuff
And the plant.
It's four feet tall now.
I raised it from a twig.
Got it at a plant sale at the supermarket
about the same time, she moved in with me.

She said she loved that plant.
She said she would care for it, keep it alive.
I found it lashed to the back deck
To keep it standing up.
Looked like it had been crucified.
The pot had no dirt in it.
Its limbs were brown, withering
The roots exposed to the sun.

Now it struggles to live.
I don't know if I should cut away the brown sections
Or just leave them for the
Plant to decide how to handle them.
It's been so damaged I don't want
to do any more damage.
The dead brown parts are still attached.
Hanging.

Every day I have coffee alone in my little nook.
The plant is next to my table now.
I look out the windows

At all the people coming and going
And I stare at my plant.
Each day it seems to urge a new
Green shoot out past the dead ones.

Let Us Breathe

We have been
suffocating for over
four hundred years.
This free-ish rope
never stopped strangling
and suspending us
in subhuman
subsistence.

We sadly watch
you step over black and
brown bodies, murdered
at the hands of brutality
choosing not to see
our free spirits dying,
gutted of hope.

Our protests are neutralized,
outcries teargassed
as you normalize
slow-motion genocide
of a once majestic people
with your silence.

Bernard Pearson

The Cowslip

Peeping from the grass
The flower that
Exhales sunshine.
Little lamp, within the mysteries
of the meadow.

Sinead Griffin

The Cormorant Comes After a Death

Black feathers dry pegged to a line of sky,
returned from a dive to the otherworld
under water. Fishing inland for winter,
as if it tastes the salt of forecast storms,

a cormorant. Perched midstream, past the footbridge
on the lower *Dodder* path, beak cocked
skywards, wings outstretched in Hallelujah pose,
marks this church of river with a cross.

An instinct stirs the bird to lift-off,
it does not fly high or far, lands over
on the other side, where walkers cannot go.
Myth has it this seabird can transport the soul,

bring back a message. In the space between us,
I hear the sound of surfaces flowing
with and past each other, river atoms gush,
matter is neither created nor destroyed.

Landing in a haven of moss and knot,
a hiding place. Set to regurgitate
by moonlight, pellets of fragment and bone.
Sadness, a fish I must swallow whole.

Crying Over Spilled Milk

Flagged down in the parking lot…

A friend's Aunt T,
(twice-removed)

Presents her with nipple guards ensconced by
sunshine yellow tissue paper in a lilac gift bag;

-Grocery carts stand in stunned silence-

Aunt T does not know that conception failed to keep;
or, that her mother's grand proclamation
omitted a step…

Once cloistered behind bedroom walls
tears deluge the cleft in her chin;

Dark circles of soured milk pool the front of
her heathered-grey tee;

Two hapless plastic guards lay unwrapped on the bed
as her nipples weep;

Wishing she could have simply said…

-Thank You-

“Sad absence of Tatar voices . . .”

Sad absence of Tatar voices

On a silent cabin porch.
In my travels I had forgotten
The language of silence.

I can’t make out that excited speech
That echoes soundlessly today,
Even though my being
Speaks to me without words.

Quietly, the land overgrows here
In ruddy *Tatarnika*. From heaven,
In a mounting storm cloud,
Zeus will thunder in Tatar.

«Тишина по-татарски печальна . . .»

Тишина по-татарски печальна
На крыльце приумолкшей избы.
Но как будто в скитаниях дальних
Я язык тишины позабыл.

Не пойму той взволнованной речи,
Что сегодня безмолвно звучит,
Хоть и мною природа в час встречи
Мне же что-то без слов говорит.

Молчаливо земля зарастает
Красноцветным татарником здесь.
А в грозу, из небес вырастая,
Прогремит по-татарски и Зевс.

Jocelyn Wright

Lost: Beautiful Lives

In 2020, so many have perished
Cherished friends, colleagues, and relatives

The main cause: structural

A lack of preparation
In relation
To investment in healthcare

Resulting in weakened infrastructures
And ruptures
In supplies and inadequate response

Detrimentally compounded by a lack of information,
Misinformation,
Even disinformation
Leading to poor choices

And governments scrambling
And citizens confused or ignoring good advice
And front line workers sacrificing

Beautiful lives
Many lost
At a cost:
They cannot be redeemed.

Sixty Back in Time

Oh Nigeria
When I think of you
I see your beauty turned into darkness
Your strength as that of a lion rested in a shamble

I see a lush green land
Manured with malnourished carcass
A land blessed with the rest
Of the devil's best

We are sixty
Should I celebrate or mourn
The decayed infrastructure or ineptitude leadership
Should I celebrate a one step forward or a hundred back in time?

Should I mourn the death?
So carelessly taken by careless leaders or
Sing my heroes passed not in vain
Hence where are the gains

You say "arise o compatriots"
With what strength should I rise
Or maybe the dead should rise
Which voice should I obey?
When all I hear is anguish and chaos

What land is my father's
When I constantly live in fear
What is love?
That which eluded when you denied me my rights
Or when tribalism robbed me of my place
And politics divided your unity

With what should I serve?
When my heart is in my hands
And the labour of my hands exploited
By the privileged few

I have cried but you have failed to listen
Now I have no tears
But to rise and to fight
For the glory of this land my land
For the freedom and liberation of my people
From the shackles of poverty
And the scavengers
That steal her wealth

I will fight until justice prevails
And our mothers can live without fear
I will fight for a strong, just, and equitable Nigeria
For the pride of the generations unborn
Not with
Love
Strength
And Might
But with all I have got.

Two Stairways

The first greets those who promenade
through the foyer to a sunken

living room; its steps—wide with
carpeted tread—ease beneath gilded panels

lined with portraits of staid patriarchs
long dead. Bright red lips brush fair cheeks,

besitos de cultura alto,
as these elegant guests' parade

through the living room past a massive
dining table and walls affixed

with innocuous ceramic buttons,
doorbell fixtures to summon the help

from the kitchen hiding a second staircase:
steep, jagged, and above all concrete.

Servants—rough hands wrapped in skin darker
than the mahogany furniture

they rub to a high shine—trudge between floors
carrying the weight of meals, loads of laundry,

flutes of lemon water, and whispered curses,
triggered by constant buzzing commands.

Meanwhile, quiet worms of hate burrow, deep
yet imperceptible, into their hearts.

The Spirit of Music Plays On

As I look at the tan shaded keys of the piano
Crackled dingy and peeling
Melodies are now memories

Of the time when elegance was about tea and piano time
When we all dressed proper and sang deep from the soul
Just as when we faced the hurricanes

We gathered at the farm
Secured the property
Gathered by the waiting piano

Until the master touched the keys
And all worries of wind and rain
Were belted out to calm the storms

And we survived
Our dear piano survived
Always leaving us with peace

Each day was another day of hope
Ballads and nursery tunes alike
Grew the spirit

Another moment to survive
Another moment to love
And as we faced the pandemic

The old soul piano was still there with us
Some have passed on
But the music remained

It comforted us as we once again gathered
And realized that all the riches of the world
Could not do more than the riches of knowing

We had each other
We still had music
We still had soul

Looking at the old piano
Abandoned by time and loss
I leave a yellow rose of joy

For time has leant more than anything else
And I am grateful for the song

Ginger Dehlinger

Ghost Trees at Midnight
(nine years after the Bear Butte burn)

Black-skinned bones
these spectral spires
shrouded in moon dust
arms akimbo
reach for the sky.

Like zombies
they prefer the dead of night
company of spirits
mask of darkness
cool, bleak silence.

Dead or half-dead
missing limbs
stripped of bark
feet planted
they refuse to topple.

A legion of ghouls
kissed by the devil
scarred
numb to the core
magnificent in moonlight.

Pangea and the First Earthquake

Nothing less than the chthonic molten forces under our feet,
so terrible and inevitable in their powers of rending,
of destruction, could have separated us.
Tearing breaking seizing everything once touching
now lost to the other. Magma's sear and push. Island isolation.
Drifting with no hope of rescue in dream after dream of
restoration
and astonishment at how perfectly you appear within them.
Wounds stretching as far back as to the breaking point
cannot heal at such distances. Oceans, salt tears, unnavigable;
the winds of change do not blow here, but howl.
Geo-logic teaches in time, that time, has no meaning.
Unmoored and unmoving, love endures.

Love the Crooked Thing
— after "Brown Penny" by Yeats

1. **A Man's Approach**

I told myself, I am too old.
And then, I am young enough.
Therefore, I spent some guineas
to find out if I could still love:

Go and love, go and love, old man,
if the woman be wise and fair. —
A guinea, a guinea, a guinea
to ruffle the roots of her hair.

2. **The Woman's Response**

He fears that he is too old
and hopes he is young enough.
Therefore, he labours plenty
to prove that he can still love.

Ah, love — come and love, old man,
for your object is lithe and bare. —
A guinea, a guinea, a guinea
to roost in the roots of my hair.

Graduate School Experiment in Group Living

We ride in silence. What else is there to say?
For more than seven months, she's lived with us,
washing his clothes, cooking all his meals,
and he gets me to drive her to the train.

For more than seven months, she's lived with us.
Lovestruck, she catered to his every need.
And he gets me to drive her to the train,
the coward. He couldn't bring himself to face her.

Lovestruck, she catered to his every need,
and yet she calls herself a feminist. —
The coward, he couldn't bring himself to face her;
some feminist she is; I think to myself.

And yet she calls herself a feminist.
I see her there, that book lying on their bed —
some feminist she is; I think to myself —
the book torn up, the front cover missing.

I see her there, that book lying on their bed.
The Feminine Mystique, very much in vogue.
The book torn up, the front cover missing,
chewed by the dog — now, there's a metaphor!

The Feminine Mystique, very much in vogue.
Washing his clothes, cooking all his meals,
chewed by the dog — now, there's a metaphor!
We ride in silence. What else is there to say?

Eftichia Kapardeli (translated by the poet)

ΑΦΗΣΕ ΜΕ

Τρυπώ το σώμα με τα κομμάτια
Του ολόγιομου Φεγγαριού
Γεμίζω το μέτωπο και τα μαλλιά σου
Με το φως του
Σε αγκαλιάζω κρυφά για να σε
Ξαναπλάσω
Να χτίσω τον Ναό της Αγάπης
Με τα πολύχρωμα φύλλα του καιρού
Και της Απολύτρωσης σου

Βαφτίζομαι στα χρώματα σου
Και μεταμορφώνομαι
Σε μια στοργή φλέβας ορμητικής νεανικής
Γίνομαι η ευλογία του φωτός
Παίρνω το σχήμα της λάμψης ……ακτινοβολώ

Χιλιάδες πουλιά της ψυχής
Γίνονται κρυψώνες ερωτικοί
Άφησε με για σένα να προσευχηθώ
Άφησε με να ντυθώ
Μαζί σου αυτή την όμορφη νύχτα
Άφθαρτο φώς

Eftichia Kapardeli (translated by the poet)

LET ME

I'm piercing the body
with
The Lunar Moon the pieces
I fill your forehead and your hair
with his light
I embrace you secretly for
to creatures you again
build the Temple of Love
with the colorful leaves of the weather
and your deliverance

I'm baptized in your colors
and I'm transforming
to an affection
vein rushing, youthful
I become the blessing of light
I get the shape of the flash ...... I radiate

Thousands of birds of the soul
They become hiding erotic
Let me pray for you
Let me get dressed
With you this beautiful night
the imperishable light

Rush of Love

Just when I was about to give up on love.
It came into my life quickly striking like a snake
but as gentle as a dove. It opened up in me passions
that I never felt before leaving me totally confused
but yet yearning for more and more. Why did love
for me take so long, this I guess I'll never know but
now that it's here finally, I'll never let it go. Forever
I'll cherish it hoping of it to never ever give it up
always savoring the sweetness from this sudden rush of love.

Dorna Hainds

dry snowflakes
a small pile
of white chrysanthemums

a foot of snow—
the white chrysanthemums
piled high

snowflakes
in all shapes and sizes—
white chrysanthemums

Kelly A. Hegi

I make room.

I am a poet. Some get it. Some don't.
Some tell me I need to hide away.
Be quiet.
Others want to talk about what I've written.
Determined to figure it out. To say where they see it.
I've learned. Readers are fickle.
I can't write for them. They will come and go.
So why write? I'm not getting paid.
The criticism is real and pointed.
Be quiet. Keep this all private.
Their words can echo.
Why write?

If I don't interpret my world, it will interpret me.
It will tell me all kinds of opinions as to who I am
What I am
How I should be
What I see and don't see
But the truth is my eyes work just fine.
I can interpret and observe the world around me through my own lens.
Possibly make sense of it.
Possibly not.

Sometimes I feel compelled, like a piece is bursting out of me.
It comes quickly, in a flash.
Others are slow and painful, a drawing out of poison.
I only see the good when I look back later.
Some that I love go unnoticed.
Some that I loathe get published.
Somehow there is room for it all.
I am a poet. That's what I do.
I make room.

Tea

I'm not interested in your Ladies Tea.
You feelin' me? Never have been. Never will be.
How is that still a thing?
Keep your skits and craft night.
Save your retreats in the wilderness.
It's like the Pastor's Wives Lunch -
an outdated and useless form designed to placate and soothe.
Plus, I'm the pastor and married to a man. So there's that.

The city is calling. Can't you hear it?
It's burning and it doesn't need tea.
It needs the life changing revolution of the Classic.
Not the Republican.
Not the Democrat.

The Classic - where women were listened to, believed and sent.
To combat hopelessness, hate and violence.
Save your tea. Unleash your women and watch this all change.

Sunday school

class action   class power
pack 'em in   for an hour
stir 'em up   non-stop
rip 'em up
rap it out   sister

He's not an easy word
God's a good chooser
chose you and me
put you here
alone

in the vastness
of this crummy basement room

and you
you must get lost
to be found
must be hurt to heal

Jesus knew about the breaks
take a look at the nail prints
in your hands

who are you
predestined Presbyterian power hour

Jesus wore scandals.

The Last Judgment

Listen for messages
Under long skirts
Of fat women.

Little ones
Hide and seek
In caverns dark
And havens safe.

Big old legs
Like Babylonian columns
Samson overthrew

In his dark
He listened to cutting messages
Under skirts.

When I Walk Upon the Earth

When I walk upon the earth,
I leave traces.
I leave traces of my being,
                    my mana.
I leave traces of my hopes,
                    my fears.
              my love
                    my soul.

Footprints,
footprints on the soil.

Breadcrumbs,
          follow them,
          follow them,
          follow them.

Follow them…
          and you will…
          and you will find me.

Censored

Lips pressed tight
Jaw set hard
Pupils wide
alert.

From the lower lip
Upward
It slides effortlessly
the string pulls taunt.

Blinded by the pain
Blinking
It pulls upward
again and again.

It's hard to breathe
Tongue tastes blood.
Rakes along the
fence of thread outside my mouth.

One, Two, Three
It's difficult to move
Eyes burn
hands are tied.

With strength from within
My lips force open
Tearing, ripping,
Standing Tall.

I am innocent but not without guilt.
I will NOT be silenced.

Annette (Wengert) Tarpley

The Mosaics of My Mind

In the Mosaics of my mind, are times both good and sad
Times when I have rejoiced, thankful for what I had
As bits and pieces of my life, have made me who I am
They lay out creating a work of art…my stories diagram

In the Mosaics of my mind, there were moments of gloom
Steadfast in my faith, my situations did not consume
For I always kept in mind…this too will eventually pass
I was strong in constitution, not fragile like broken glass

In the Mosaics of my mind, I knew who I would become
A woman who can withstand storms, my eye on the rising sun
I am capable of compassion, I can feel another's pain
I can find joy in other's happiness, and what in life they gain

In the Mosaics of my mind, I abhor prejudice and hate
I believe one has control of their destiny and fate
Never one to like toxicity, I prefer a harmonious life
One that I can happily enjoy, not laden with the burden of strife

In the Mosaics of my mind, I am content in who I have become
I want to positively impact another's life before each day is done
I want to live each day to its fullest, something new each day to find
I want others to fondly remember me, when it becomes the end
of my time

September 3rd 2020

Your words wash over me like a soft river current in summer
I feel them but they go around me quiet and steady
We are all so similar it would seem
Common agonies and joys surround me
It is not quite boredom
As intellectuals complicate simplicity
I feel underneath
Cradled by dirt and grass
Under fallen leaves in autumn
Ready to go deeper
Underground
To be among rich soil and tree roots
Damp minerals will absorb into me until I
Become the earth in winter
Massive and spinning
Only to thaw
Melt and evaporate in spring
The ocean and sky
Will swell and breathe
Releasing me
To the infinite beyond
I am becoming
So free
Your words become me

Lament of the Pando Aspen

Utah's Trembling Giant
sends urgent pleas to roots
meant to mother saplings.

Inside the trees' dappled bark
phloem carries spats of sugars
down shrinking stems
where sunburnt shoots dry;

I dodge in and out of shade
sun pouring past quaking leaves
flames of orchid, mariposa

a doomed understory
to the hundred-acre spread
—47,000 trees.

The Pando's cloned body
not singing ancient songs
of growth and harmony.

Now the dry leaves mourn
aching for cool rain to ease
the thirst of brittle heartwood.

Joan Canby

Summoned

Her portraits -- a brunette in crimson,
a Hollywood pose, slight smile, nursed

with family ambition, marriage pedigree --
today lie covered, hidden by her children

in a basement, in a cloak closet, in a garage.
Haughty, spoiled, The Belle, my Mother,

taught us to run for her, summoned
us to fetch, to obey, to hear her words,

Here's something you can do for me.
Once we lived amongst citrus orchards

below mesquite-dry mountains and acres
of cattle grazing. We heard in early

morning the sounds of sea lions barking,
foghorns protecting fishermen trawling

for holy halibut, Garibaldi, mackerel. To
call us in from our freedom, my Mother

reached for a foghorn. Each child given
a code to know it was their time to return

to her. Mine a three short foghorn blast.
When bulldozers took our orchards, cattle

sold, silver packed into cedar, mahogany
chests, alongside the foghorn, I packed to

boarding school, then her portraits hung
in smaller splendor. Later I left to become

not like her. Until the hospital visits, the
weeks coordinated to tend, to bring breakfast

trays, count out pills, wait for her to need
me. Bundled in a soiled gown, in a room

with a view of climbing Cecile Brunner
roses, reduced to a house the size of our

ranch's barn in a community once a dairy
field, I brought her home after another

surgery. She grumbled, *I want an adult*
beverage. Soon a blast shook the thin walls

to the roof of the condo. Our retriever
howled. The dogs in the community barked.

The widow next door feared an earthquake,
fire, civil unrest. I ran with black Labrador

in tow down stairs fearful of possible harm
into my Mother's room to hear, *I take ice*

in my Vodka, and saw the reappearance
of the foghorn. Then the next shifts, my

brother, my sister arrived for another round
of trays, adult beverages and response to a

foghorn's bidding. As our shifts continued,
each of us brought her a bell to woo her

from her foghorn. My brother gave her a
Greek ceramic bell. My sister an Irish

Waterford crystal. I gave her a silver bell
with a plea, *Mother here is a bell,* I *can*

hear it, use it, I'll come. Each visit a
bouquet of bells stayed on her nightstand,

next to the TV control, empty Vodka glass
and foghorn. Until the day we weren't

summoned, until, she was.

Games

The meaning of life is a good companion. - Carl Jung

I like people who like games, my mother announced creating family life within the pitch and toss. Every Saturday I rode my bicycle to the golf club a bathing suit under my shorts to jump into the lake between holes. Carrying my grandfather's wooden clubs: his nib lick, mashie, driver and putter, I won my first tournament at 12. Once before a swimming meet, sick with nerves, vomiting beside the pool, I pleaded with my mother not to compete. *You will compete*, she said. At home in my father's den a trophy case held the loving cup trophies of my mother, father, grandfather from country clubs in California, Marrakesh and Philadelphia. I'd practice my tennis every afternoon hitting balls on the garage door, then practiced my putting in the backyard pitch and putt on our lawn. Games filled the cupboards, television programs were turned on to national and international tournaments. Games were our conversations. While other families went to church on Sundays, I drove a golf cart and practiced my short game with my parents.

I stopped playing games, retreated to books, to solitary walks to become different. In college I took an Intensive Latin Workshop at Berkeley, staying at the International House on Telegraph Avenue. At dinner, sitting with a Japanese student studying English, we talked about golf, Japan. On his expense account, we went to dinner every Saturday night eating cracked crab at Fisherman's Wharf, fettucine con scampi in North Beach, then Irish coffees at Buena Vista Cafe. Every other Saturday we'd go to a Japanese restaurant in the city for miso soup, teriyaki, yakatori and soba. We shared our dreams. One day you'll be president of Sumitomo Bank, I told him. *One day you will be a published writer*, he told me. I'd quote Basho, *go to the pine to learn from the pine*, Catullus, *amare homines est bonum*. Every Sunday morning, we played golf in the Berkeley Hills. I'd call out, look there is a deer! He'd stop, watch the rustling in the bushes, as fog lifted off for the vista of the Bay like a ribbon of lace. He'd call from the opposite side of the fairway, *Beautiful shot. You're on the green,* -- golf our pas de deux. Every Saturday at the elevator my Samurai friend bowed as I thanked him for dinner returning a bow.

One Saturday, Italian and German engineers asked to join our Sunday morning game. Divided by teams, I with my tall Samurai friend and the Italian and the German in the other team. My friend with his strong swing as wide and elegant as a samurai sword swept through grass, never sliced the ball, to land in the center of the fairway. Annoyed with losing, the engineers watched our dance, left out and beaten. At the last hole, the German, stocky, blond, square-jawed asked me, *what is your family, English*? I answered, three-fourths English and a fourth from the Scottish Highland clan of MacDonald of Glengarry. Nodding towards my friend, blunt as a blade, *why are you with him*?

Paul Sherman

The Tire

On grueling ascent, rock-hopping
turbulent creek with hope to reach
the waterfall by noon, I wonder,
did I choose the wrong prong,
navigating boulders, before basking
in mist of waterfall.
I listen to birdsong, observe spruce
towers in formation until the sun
indicates time for descent.
I find the tire creekside below the falls.
It stands upright, wedged in stone with tread
possessing deep valleys, the sidewall reads:
Airplane Tire. US Air Force. I jot the model
number down for research.
The tires from a C47 cargo plane
used by the military in WWII.
The Evening Independent reveals tragedy:
5 October 1949. The plane departs D.C.
destined for Alabama, crashes
into Mt. Mitchell under heavy fog.
Rescuers find charred wreckage days
after the crash. All nine airmen are dead.
One man crawled away from wreckage
and was burned.
In a summer dream I climb to the fall in fall;
hear before I see the roar of propellers,
shining fuselage shave ridge top trees.
Silver plane soar over autumn vale
of nine doomed men.

Cold Open Window

Those invincible jackets, saviour of the universe
Cracking salted jokes on the idle, aside
The circular references catching the burn
By Spoiling one's duty through a comatose breeze
Behaving strangely on the ordinary time.

Embarrassed for a time, reaping the hurricane
Feeling entitled for want of a better stance
Being honest at a cost, secrets gone explosive
The anaesthetic of television wherever seen
Watered, left to dry, too advanced for some.

Higher hair, closer to God. Wishing to be used
The bizarre record sleeves go forth infinitely
Closer to a saviour to pick up and go.
Seated outside to scrag the multitudes medicine
Sucking carbohydrates through a napkin dearly.

The convenient public, surveying more than necessary
Given ultimate shocks catching in full view,
Burning entitlement where most gone before
Lapping up design under a broken sign
Sleeping until Christmas a favourite pastime.

Drizzled into a cul-de-sac, turned around spite,
Working into cemeteries a typical forthcoming
Never giving up on beloveds, laughed at,
Seated and entertained like always before
The glorious hypocrisy of staying sane.

Priscilla Webster-Williams

Poem after Ferlinghetti's

Be a poet or a researcher.

Be a poet
or paint a tea pot.
Get out, go roundabout,
be a troubadour
in a Chevy, Subaru or Saab.
Fish rivers for bass.
Make up stories, yodel songs,
or harvest the scuppernong.

Be a traveler, see America
with a camera.
Salute each day, face
it with coffee, tea, or decaf.
Praise sun and stars. Address
others kindly. Plant seeds.
Be a flower gardener
or a computer nerd.

Do what you love.
Learn, evolve.
Play tennis,
or write a sonnet.
Open your laptop,
explore new portals,
look for kin or a twin.
Don't be a nitwit,
celebrate quirks
this is humanity's circus.

Raise Georgia peaches,
or guard sheep.
Make a messy salad, cube
meat for a BBQ.
Grill a steak,
read some Keats.
Wear vintage
clothes or open a gate,
get out of the closet.
Celebrate the solstice.
Create a Tebalfla
Alphabet,
or devise a system
for mystics.

Go to mosque or a church
(unless there's a crunch.)
Pray,
strum a harp.
Search for saints,
look to the mountains.
The Blue Ridge Mountains—
a smoky league of saints!

Know yourself. Follow your star.
Denounce hatred, racism, political rats.
Evoke
your own voice.
Be a poet
or paint a perky tea pot.

Priscilla Webster-Williams

At Timberlake Earth Sanctuary

Lying on a plank of wood, I wanted to push
my fears and anxieties onto the trees
standing near, but I could not lose them
until I noticed the under-side of green leaves,
and mottled, brighter ones above,
swaying in the canopy.

The plank of wood became a place of death
for what troubled me, and as I shed
my worried self, the trees began to stir
and whisper— and I knew I had been changed
by an upside-down world of visions.

In the Arms of the Ocean

Next to this ocean of unsung peace
Recalling days gone by, each a wave
Distinct on the rise, merged on descent.
Salty air clears my head; sun toasts my
skin
Like facing a fire in winter.

Wading at the water's edge, waves
spread
Around my feet, then retreat
Pulling sand away, exposing coquinas
Who quickly burrow between my toes,
Returning to safety
Deep below.

As I walk into the rolling roar
Waves collapse against my legs,
Pushing me away, even as I advance.
But underneath, they tug me forward--
Sand constantly shifting on the ocean
floor.
In this way, the moon speaks to the
earth.

I fall in the warm saltwater.
Weightless, I float
Like the place found gazing into a
lover's eyes.
Pulse quickening and desire rising,
Dizziness so sweet,
The ground moves beneath our feet.

Sea Legs, 2020

Unmoored in oceans
of possibility,
swept up in the tide
of a rising storm.

Now is the time
to plant your feet,
engage your core
and mind your alignment:
    Head over heart.
    Heart over hips.
    Hips hinged over knees.
    Knees flexed for balance,
    and ready for prayer.

Let the howling winds rage
and the raging waters swell.
Let the ship pitch and heave
through roiling waves and troughs
to find safe port on some unknown shore.

Below the churning surface
and above the angry sky
there are deeper currents flowing
undisturbed, unnoticed, unwavering --

a quiet place to anchor head and heart
while you weather this convulsive sea.

Mary Kay Fruga

A Poem about Snakes

Today I am thinking about snakes,
living always aligned with the earth,
bodies smooth and sinuous,
movement graceful, supple, certain.

Seeking shelter and food, the warmth of the sun,
raising their young as every creature does --
except for the burden of derision.

What is it like
to meet contempt and fear at every turn?
No words to speak,
just a forked tongue lashing out
at an unforgiving history.

Already in this early spring
I cast a wary glance across my yard,
suspicious of dark corners,
of innocent piles of leaves warming,
of every hole in the ground or chink in the foundation.
Old fears in a new season
of an ancient creature, all muscle and grace.

I see something slithering:
          How do you move
          from dread to deference,
          from alarm to admiration?

Stay close to the earth.
Keep silent.
Rest whenever you can
on a warm rock
in the sun.

Michael Gaspeny

Tribute to My Former Hygienist

Beneath the clock with toothbrush hands,
a photo of her Black Lab glowing in green grass.
My Retriever slept with paws on my ribs.
We spoke of how we loved them,
though they scarfed rot and vaulted fences—
a miracle they survived their drives.

She tapped the teeth that didn't have long,
gave me a little brush to scour the gums.
Once, after being flossed, I pointed
to her wedding picture, saying,
What a striking couple!
Clicking notes into her computer,
she said, *He's with another woman now.*
But he drops by. I let him in.
We claw the walls and moan 'God!'
I will never say again,
'Hold me a little longer.'

I said, *Asking becomes begging.*
She added, *Begging becomes death.*
We laughed.

At the next appointment,
her replacement bubbled,
How was your Christmas?
I almost asked.

Archive

the stubbornness
Borrowed.
The prayers
Unanswered.
The color of the blood, blue
Tragic.
The palpitating heart
Goodbyes.
Half lived silence
Pauses.
A life lived between two ends
A fabrication of two stories
All exchanged in a
Heartbeat.

Frank Doonan

Dragons, Villains and Spies

Dragons, Villains and Spies.
Mom and Dad have gone to town!
the dragons and villains are about!
time to rally the heroes at the barn!

Mount red and white Schwinn steed!
Charging down the driveway
with plans and schemes of heroes deeds
slaying dragons and defeating evil ways

Red cape flapping in the wind
high wheelies and ramp jumps
playing card jet motors roaring
skids in the gravel humps
black Mack snapping at my tires

Heroes gather in the hay loft
Glow in the dark decoder rings
Flashed from beneath caps
Passwords guard against evil spies in disguise
Lookouts report approaching enemy

The evil swans and geese stalking
cat's eyes spy from the dark loft
the menacing paper wasps circling
plans of attacks whispered in hay tunnels and ramparts
the unseen evil villains in shadows lurking

The feed lot searched for ammunition
some cow pies wet and nasty
mud balls and mule turds hard and round
burlap bags loaded carefully

Dragon swans and evil geese repulsed
villains in the shadows return
the evil attack repelled
the heroes mount ramparts triumphant

Black Max panting and tired
torn jeans and cow pie and dung ball wounds
stripped and hosed in the front yard
with dreams for another victorious day.

Margaret Bockting

No Telling

"STAPLES 2 HB" indents one panel. This
pencil's six orange sides lead to a metal clasp
followed by a flattened red eraser. (Much of what
was written disappeared.) At the other end
where the paint's been shaved, the wood narrows
toward the central graphite—not a point here, just a blunt
dark possibility.

Margaret Bockting

Lumber

lumber (verb) – move in a slow, heavy, awkward way; cut and prepare forest timber for transport and sale; heap together in disorder.
lumber (noun) – timber or logs dressed for use.

In neighborhood after neighborhood,
inside every wall of every house,

you are the skeleton—O felled and fallen, hauled
to sawmills and sent forth! You raise up

the possibility of excluding the extremes.
And we remain indebted, too, to you

for chairs and tables, desks, shelves, the doors
to almost everything. Above these rooms

you carry the shingles' weight, beyond these rooms
the weight of shadows

who paddle between shores. O forests forgive
our greed. You lie here beneath my pen.

You curl in millions of layers
wound tightly, poised by every toilet. We

have woven you through our history;
battered, broken, burned you.

We witness the catastrophe of your disappearance, yet
consume, consume. O mourn

for yourselves
and the enormous waste we tread.

Little Life

Here, in this poem, the deep in my heart
calls to the deep inside you.
Do you not see, beloved, how earth
teaches us the language of sorrow?
The collective gloom, deep as Baobab roots,
spreads over our heads like a sky.
We all have wailed over loss.
O, how the misfortune of one
corrupts the fortune of another.
The dead. We all have buried our dead.

On the ill-fated day of the crash
that transformed my friend into a ghost,
all the gods, bereft of their saving power, looked on.
What is a god but a self-made answer for our curiosity?
Do you not see—
how we hackney their names into reality?
If the Lord be Lord, let him deliver me from
the multitude of my griefs.

There is no respite in the world.
And darkness, as a vesture,
covers our totality.
This my little life,
so certain of uncertainty.

To the Ancestors

May I be the drum.
O, let the earth beat me with all its grief—
the drumsticks of gloom slapping my hide—
but may I still remain the origin of dance.

When Satan slaughtered the Saviour,
it wasn't a slaughter. And Joseph
in a dried-up well will come to mean
Joseph seated in Pharaoh's kingdom.

O, let me claim
what was sent to claim me.
Let the world beat me with all its woes
but let me not be brittle or broken.

Instead of silence, let there be rhythm.
O, let me melody through melancholy.

In the day that grief will arise with its army,
may grief never prevail.

May I be the drum
still breathing joy.

Tuur Verheyde

Bird's Eye View

The struggle strikes at dusk's first light,
Ferociously hacking away at our pallid flesh.
Claw marks carve a blueprint in our skin.
Limbs are severed at the base.
At the threshold of our back,
It harpoons into the spine.
The wall is breached,
Grey matter sets the lower levels ablaze.
Words are made manifest in the nerves, no abstracts here.
Regret, a hissing itch,
Fear, gallstones throbbing,
Loss slithering through the veins
For guerrilla strikes of phantom pain.
Then pain is soil and skies above,
Pain is all.
The stars look down and all they see…
Worms writhing in the dirt,
Dust rising in an empty room.

A May Day

(for Rich Rice)

The screen near my desk window is ajar;
white locust and black cherry petals
blow over my keyboard,
onto books, my journal, the floor.

I imagine every window and door
wide open to this day:
jays, sparrows, cardinals, and doves
fly in to sing and make nests;
squirrels hunt for nuts and
find hiding places.

My magic crystal
prisms sunlight into ribbons;
it dapples the walls
and paints my hands.

Up and down the stairwell
blue-purples, golds and greens,
reds and pinks shimmer
rainbow tickertape.

But I have just put down the phone:
our friend died this morning,
blessedly at peace we learned,
a few hours before we called.
A dear, good life vanished from us!

We wish him to be forever
embraced by such a day as this:

every part of it as full of light
as clear mountain lake water
reflecting trees and sky,
sounding its music,
bringing into presence a
great circle of loved ones.

Nancy Corson Carter

A Healing of Memory

...perhaps all the dragons of our lives are princesses who are only waiting to see us once beautiful and brave. Perhaps everything terrible is in its deepest being something helpless that wants our help.

-Rainer Maria Rilke, a letter

So small and saggy,
this unsmiling child in the photograph
clutches a sand bucket with plump hands.
Her father has returned from three years at war,
a stranger who steals her mother's love.
Soon she will have a new sister
whose laughter will mock her heaviness;
she will misunderstand her sadness as a wrong.

She cannot swim in the creek behind her;
she is frightened by the cold, deep currents.
She hates her fear, she hates her slowness;
she wishes she were large and armored.
She does not know how much she wants to be held;
she does not know how much she will
give herself away,
year after year, desiring to lose forever
this child she despises.

Three decades later
I return to this place in the photo.
There on the chill stones, the coarse beach,
I show this child how the water mirrors her beauty.

I show her the pleasure of swimming
with strong, graceful motion.

I show her her fears:
they are dragons become princesses
That dark reservoir she could not empty
now drains dry and fills with light.
I tell her "You are my child;
I love you."

Steve Cushman

The Accident

Driving home from
dinner, we passed the
wreckage; the top of
the silver Civic gone,
a white sheet covering
the front seat. How many
were there? One, two?
We didn't know.

We'd fought quietly
during dinner, over
the kids and who should
have mowed the yard
and other perceived slights
and then we were driving
along I-40 and saw what
we saw. You set your hand
on mine, squeezed, and
we drove like that the
rest of the way home.

Kristine Chalifoux

Winter Aquarelle

A mid-December dusk
Inks the sky, a muted watercolor

Muffling whatever small triumph
Of color the day had tried to paint.

Silhouetted against the grey, the trees' empty branches
Strike stark poses against the darkening canvas

While wind flings handfuls of rain against windows--
When was the last time we made love?

Tonight there will be no symphony of storm
No Bach concerto or something by Chopin --

Only a small winter squall, tears, an empty kettle
And ashes, grey and cold, in the grate.

Trench Warfare

How much space is there now between us?
Not just the physical geography of distance

But the cartography of absence
That stretches taut from coast to coast

The space where the words that once
Buoyed us now net us like a drowning man

Clutching the lifeguard so tightly both men
Go under. Living with you was like living

With my hands around a live grenade.
All the time we soldiered forward

Unwilling to throw ourselves on the landmine
Of divorce I tried to find a way to keep

You from pulling the pin. Or maybe I just
Needed to feel like your savior. Maybe

You needed me to be the one
The water boarder trying to get you to speak

Or the shadowy figure behind you
The one working the interrogation

Lights to cast your shadow larger than
Life on the wall behind you

Or better yet the one who mistakes
the shadow for the man himself.

Virtue, Versus Forgiveness

As all are, I was born into slavery.
The world held me captive.
By being good and virtuous
I tried to find peace and freedom,
To escape from guilt and shame.
Still my errant thoughts ran wild
within the fence of justice. Efforts
to break free caused scars, not release.
Shame and guilt embittered my soul,
As bitter as quinine on the tongue.
Unhappiness and regret burdened
My defenseless spirit, regularly.
Each morning I awoke to defeat.
If I did better than my peers,
Pride defeated me even then.
Even human love was tainted
For my beloved was as I am,
A slave within the confines
Of the stockyard of life.
His love could free neither of us,
though we were as privileged as others
With food, water, and shelter.
Physically we did not suffer lack.
The fences protected us from predators, but
The distant green pastures were denied us,
Until forgiveness, requested, was given and
For a season, satisfied my desire, until
Rebellion and anxiety returned to my heart.
My spirit chafed under failure, regret, confusion.
Unlovely, disgusting to myself, unable to best
Boundaries of my miserable enslavement, my
Freedom came unexpectedly one day.

My Redeemer came, said, “I love you.”
though I did not love myself, I accepted
His gift, faith. Faith enabled me to
Believe His word and trust His promise.
Restrictions to my spirit vanished
At last, I am free. Forevermore!

Louise Runyon

Medlock school powwow, 1988

on Earth Day the Native Americans came and reordered
pushed back the straight lines of tables and chairs
drew a huge circle of chalk on the floor
ignored report cards and rulers, made the world round
teachers and parents, principals and children
sat on the floor together in a circle –
the change, profound

inside the circle Jonathan Warrior did the hoop dance
twenty hoops encircling his neck and his limbs –
he juggled and balanced them, stood on one foot
he threw them and caught them, turned all around
he jumped in the air, the children were rapt –
then one hoop began to fall, and another –
the hoop dance fell apart, the hoops
lay on the ground

the MC for the day, William Eagle Hurt, said
that is how it is, children, sometimes
things fall apart

and he started to cry

there was surprise, a hush
as William remembered
his own falling apart
the children, the alcohol, all that was lost

a grown man crying
the children learned more on that round day
than on all the rectangular, triangular
arrow-straight days
before

On the Sixth Anniversary
Of My Son's Death

The grey clouds streak across the October sky
Sweeping out the last of June with a swirl of
Dead leaves and dried grass.

The chill will come soon.
The trees will gracefully bend and sigh
To the wind's whispering wishes
Shaking their leafy hold
----- "LET GO!"

Let go

The seasons change without knowing why
And Winter always
waits

Your twenty years was
Blessed with Love and
Grace,

Enough to last

Forever
And Time steps aside
To let me softly weep.

Marc Puricelli

The Ephemeral

Follow the frozen molecule of water
Balancing on the edge of a snowflake
Wafting up in the draft to
Suddenly whoosh down and
Settle unharmed and unheard,
Waiting to be Beautiful
If only for a moment ----
Then melting in place with
A kiss from the sun.

We don't lose our innocence just once,
But always

Bougainvillea

My fingertips, scented
And nectar sweetened, feted in
Dry season blossoms, tender and
And spike shorn; split raw with familiar ache;
Bougainvillea-ed. The blooms, bold and vining
Petals skyward pointing, as if praying or votive,
The way humans yearn for beauty, avid and
Ravenous, like a candle lit and flickering
Races to burn itself out, eager, I pluck at them
And leave bits of myself, human sacrifice
For the perennial altar, because beauty rarely
Leaves you unscathed when she touches you, she
Splits you open, tender soft like new birth,
A sacred thing.

Wreathe

For another brief September,
The Cirsium are in bloom again and
I am reminded that someone I loved is gone.

With their abrupt flamboyance,
They garland the landscape with these
Perennial and rampant generosities

Proof that no walls can hold
Against the wayward meandering of so called weeds;
Extracts tended by nature's own hand, wreathing the world

In unasked for beauty.
Their brief and sudden effusions no less luminous,
No less consequential for having been short lived.

And here again for another brief October
The Cirsium are in bloom,
And I am reminded that you are gone.

Paul Brookes

When All the World Are Ghosts

and you are brought up walking through walls,
floating in midair to disappear in sunlight,

to become a solid is a weight of grief.
I must walk around objects,
that if I hit will tumble fall and break.

I knew my old life was gone
when I walked into a wall,
bloodied my nose and grazed my knees.

I can hold my favourite vase.
I am hungry all the time.

In sunlight I bathe.
I cannot see my mam and dad,
or old friends. Ghosts are a myth
in this solid world.

Glenn Cassidy

Like the Lid to the Takeout Coffee

Deceptively simple in engineering,
the frail plastic sticks to the stack
in the silvery dispenser, easily tears
while twisting it free or snapping it
into place with its partner.
See-through thin, yet it dams
the boiling tide many times its mass,
braces the floppy container like truss work,
holds the crushable sides rigid,
as powerful and ephemeral as
I love you.

Glenn Cassidy

Paper

At one past midnight the women kiss,
holding high the paper
that curls in the damp air,
city hall aglow with a thousand candles.
Paper, by custom the gift at year one
in the parade of leather and fruit,
metals and jewels –
gold should they make a half-century.
Paper, a year early,
the lone page costs less than a night out.
Paper, many years late,
a price paid in briefs and argument,
relatives only,
parent or guardian only,
and much, much, paper.
No future gift can bring as many riches
to the two women
or the hundreds of Massachusettans
stamping their feet to keep warm
in the cold plaza,
applauding, crying, witnessing,
as the two women pause atop the marble steps
and hold high the paper.

The Harlot

I sit in the corner of the Sazerac Bar
and watch them
These people who picnic in cemeteries
and drink milk punch for brunch and have all variety of vices
And they all exist very well
with not a nit of care for how others do
So content are they within their hazy minds
Suckling slow and easy
from the licentious bosom of a harlot
named New Orleans

The Sound of End of Summer

I hear the sound of end of summer
fireflies hitching rides on rivers
children's eyes
slow the ebb of lofty dreams
freedom rings in no color
they know not of the broken brazen
flagellating men and women
licking at the boots of power
binding gagging Jesus
editing a declaration
fucking with a crucifix
cum stains on a fragile mattress
ticking stitched of teeth and bones
and dreams and striving to be better
red and white and blue
stolen by the Maga
hatred hearted
let the world be damned
care not for the future of the children
let them eat from the palm of Nero
sipping from his leaded chalice
hurry let me relish one more moment
before truth and hope are gone forever
bring back to me the dream of Dr. Martin Luther King Jr.
and Framers flawed and fragile
beating insouciant in the hearts of our children's laughter
let me relish this for one more moment
before they force us to forget
I hear the end of summer

Adirondack Chair

Jigsaw puzzle of greenery, the trees
Nestle next to each in the
slicing sideways light of sunset.
The yard in the back is filled with it,
Filled with the late late summer side slant
of sun,
The plastic Adirondack chairs, left, as we left them,
Me, looking at you, maybe my feet
in your lap...
No, it wasn't us that set them ajar.
The one time we sat there, your discomfort
Grated on my tranquil storybook
Vision, of us sitting
in the sun,
Drinking,
The Wine,
so we went inside.

Now I see them, those pretend plastic,
Pale blue, light blue to match
The house,
chairs of ease,
One chair looking at the other, while
the other stares off into
Space.
We meant to build a fire that
Summer, a fire pit
evening of
Romance.
But, I saw your dis-ease.
Was it the heat? The drone
of the bugs?
The chance of a gnat,
Landing in your
drink?

Or was it,…something
Different.
Something not found
in the sideways slant of
cooling air.
Was it, something
else, off
in that horizon,
Blocked
by the pale blue, the light
Blue house.
Something,
cutting your sight
Off
from the road.

It must have been, because, you said
Goodbye, several times
That summer. A nod, a
kiss, and you were
Off,
in your mind,
because you never
left, but sat in your uncomfortable
Sadness of not
Belonging here, or
Where you thought;
Wistful plans set, a
Blaze, not by
Midnight cords of wood
in a pile among the
Rocks,
Set ablaze by whimsy,
A promise, not
Promise.

Deborah T. Johnson

So, we sat that summer
and watched the flowers in the
pots bloom,
and the rains carry one
away,
And the gnats gnatting
as gnats do,
Cannon balling into pinot,
taking up
Residence, in that
Pale blue, light blue
house
With plastic mountain
Chairs
On the lawn.

Those chairs,
Those, Adirondack chairs
Still sit, still sit askew, still
sit, in the slanting light,
Still sit, waiting,
as I do,
For a time
Things, will be right
with the
World.
We must get, to
the other side, of
That Summer.
Let the snow pile high,
on those Chairs,
Get to, the whimsy, and
the Promise.
Watch down the
road, for a time to
travel, and not sit,
in uncomfortable
Sadness,
Askew in plastic
Chairs.

Jerry Judge

Luna Moth

Three nights in a row
it clings to the screen.
I can't understand.
One dazzling week to live

yet it's lured to eternity
by artificial lights.
I turn the cabin to darkness
so we can take flight.

Mary Elmahdy

For Boppa

Gather my thoughts,
gather them all to me.
Let me paw through them
searching for that secret remedy.
If I could only collect that lost
intuition scattered around me.

Bursting out of the house
I ran smack into the smell of spring
walked into it to befriend a tree
with her ash limb bending so gracefully;
bent to meet my melt, hands grabbing
as I went falling into the deep, deep. . .

nearly forgotten,
early-post-verbal
ocean of childhood
where the world seemed so wide,
so tall, like my first love the ancient oak,
our closest neighbor to the East
appearing more beautifully weathered even
than my grandfather.
Strong, rooted, negotiating with the heat.

Grandpa, pop, bop, Boppa.
Boppa stuck.
The papa of our maternal line,
the son of a Mang mother
who lived on Mang Avenue
where we spent bucolic Sundays
after Mass, after the sacraments,
and the washing of our hands.

Mary Elmahdy

It's well I remember Boppa rocking
his chair creaking as we played
like an old Adirondack bone
with a titch of the lumbago
puffing on his corn cob
gazing off all the way back to over there
in dignified quietude
dressed in Sunday's suit
beneath the full autumnal offering
of seed, the long black beans of the catalpa
as long as the summer's day
hanging above him like jewelry
for the Queen of Bavaria
before plummeting down to earth,
to the pungent smell of the loam he built up
over six decades of fertilizing the old way
compost rotting sickeningly sweet
cooking in the late summer's heat
heavy like a blanket for the cold
good for the plums and the concord vines
and the catalpa tree
the best shade tree
I will ever fall for
falling down on my back
to watch the fireflies dance in the lily-pad-leaves of the catalpa.

Jonathan Giles

Resurrection

The notice reads as if Ed Roach died yesterday—
the family asking everyone to celebrate the life of their 24-year-old son.

Oh, plow the red clay, yellowed leaf.

A black man in the county back in 1920, Ed was beaten, shot five times, and strangled
for attacking a white woman on the road to town.

Dig beneath the loblolly and sweet gum.

Working with his family in the tobacco since sunrise,
a mob of 200 men judged otherwise, hung him from an old oak at the AME church.

Ed Roach, rise with your hanging rope.

In the red-dawn hours, his family cut him down, buried their child in the bright leaf.
They burned the oak, a flaming epitaph on the road to town.

Your time hidden in the fields is over.

The service is like a shock from a live wire—
a current singeing us all in the county, exposing the simmering rot within.

Dear Flower Girl

Dear Flower Girl
With a Smile so beautiful
Get Ready for the storm
But Never Fear
And Embrace the Thunder
The lightning and the Rain
Which will help you bloom.

Wildflowers

She hoped to become
Free as those Wildflowers
Nourished by the love of Mother Nature
To grow and bloom
But in that moment of
Torment, despair and Wounds
He plucked her petals
Instead of watering her.

Bed of Lavenders

Earth as her pillow
Stars as her blanket
She sleeps in a bed of lavender
Sounds of nature as a discreet lullaby
Singing her to sleep
So peaceful, so pure, so untamed.

Phil Venable

In Case I Do Not Mention

Birthing me
Reducing my old skin for sacrifice
Standing again for you
Trembling, the air I breathe
Laughing
Tumbling out
Flesh made word from your lips
Your hair cut short into brunette flowers

In case I do not mention.

Man's life

In memory of our dear Delaney Watson

A force of heart and guts
Caring shimmering through
Strife rife with life
Determined live - and - do

Hell, high water and adversity
Endless cycles joy and despair
Acceptance resignation revival
Life indeed not fair

Flames and dark shroud
Blazing righteous indignation
Standing tall in torment
Insistent on repudiation

Of wrongs made into truths
Lies into standard of being
Love distorted into agony
Of involuntarily seeing

A light that is from darkness
A promise painfully thwarted
A vision abruptly unseen
A destiny never started

His path extended vigorously
Despair set aside relocated
Blessings unseen accepted
Life passionately consummated

Sore Loser

First the sky lets loose a cloud, then slices the black sky thin into soft wisps of rain. Suddenly I am drowning in the emptiness of shadows; the silence of being alone. Chill wraps around me. I sink into the cold shoulders of midnight blues. As the night drags on, the hole within me deepens; a hollow sound, the echo of moonlight disappearing into the sea.

It is an odd thing, to fall in love with Winter; the realization moments are now memories, a beautiful tragedy. No fate worse than death, except in the living left, grieving the loss of what was, what will never be. It appears I am the Autumn leaf, bereft of color. Frozen at the foot of your tree. Forgotten by all parts of you, a distant memory. A sore loser, I've lost it all. Hope all is well with you and you had a Merry Christmas. Wishing you a happy new year. Stay safe and I will talk to you soon.

Nadine Hayes

Oblivion

The night calls.
I can hear its whispers in my sleep,
feel my head sink deep
into the soft pillow of its tongue,
the language of darkness.
I wonder if I should wake.
After all, there is so much comfort
in the quiet,
the nothingness.

Catch 22

I catch
better than I release.

Always the umpire.
Never the pitcher.

I hold on
when I should let go.

Forgive me
if I don't fall for you

like the leaves do
in the Autumn breeze.

It's not that easy
to surrender

when the trust fall
left you in pieces.

Rural Myth

After I skate off the last edge, bump into rough treatment,
fall off the cliff, the steady thump of boots-to-trail awakens
that spark, as I push up through bedrock, a lakebed
awaiting, through rocks, some shale, to start my frantic
swim to the surface where air stimulates: I feel the cold
water once life returns, but what did I learn buried so far,
sniffing the salt caves, alone at my age, noticeably nude
as I beat hypothermia to the leaf-barren trees, not yet
budding in the brisk new spring? Is there a precocious four
leaf clover rising at Onanda, the pine tree girl's camp
turned into pristine, simple, non-electrified cabin resort? Is it
quick to be lost, cherished then missed by the heart of an
11-year-old boy, who, not having pets, wants to preserve it,
the fruition of a joke come true? "I see a four-leaf clover,"
he says, then reaches down and finds one to pick at once.
He's not afraid to hand it to me, but, embarrassed by nudity,
I hand it back, borrow a towel, scamper to shelter, try to
find a phone, to remember the number of someone I knew
thirty years ago who might give up their sail, fish, swim,
trilobite hunt to take a funny trip to a clothing store, for starters.

Maryam Abassi is an Indian citizen who is currently a student as well an academician. Surrounded by literature and her love for poetry is what she looks forward to in life.

Kolawole Adebayo, a former poetry reader at Feral Journal, is a Nigerian poet with works published in several journals around the world. His chapbook manuscript, *INVOCATIONS*, was recently selected by Kwame Dawes and Chris Abani for the New-Generation African Poets Chapbook Box-Set Series (Akashic Books, 2021).

Adebimpe Oluwafunmilayo Adeyemi is a poet, writer and lawyerwho loves to tell hardlytold stories with her pen. When she isn't writing or lawyering, she is to be seen traveling and adventuring.(Editor, HC VIII)

Akin-Ademola Emmanuel is a gifted writer who uses literature as a handtool to stir souls towards critical issues. His works have appeared or are forthcoming in Cón-sciò, Nantygreens, parousia, Kalahari Review, Active muse, Christopher Okigbo anthology and elsewhere.

Karren LaLonde Alenier is author of eight poetry collections—including *Looking for Divine Transportation,* winner, 2002 Towson University Prize for Literature; *The Anima of Paul Bowles* and *how we hold on* (new). Her poetry and fiction have been published in *Mississippi Review*, *Jewish Currents*, and *Poet Lore*. Visit Alenier.blogspot.com.

Dee Allen: African-Italian performance poet based in Oakland, California. Active on the creative writing & Spoken Word tips since the early 1990s. Author of 5 books [*Boneyard, Unwritten Law, Stormwater* and *Skeletal Black,* all from POOR Press, and from Conviction 2 Change Publishing, *Elohi Unitsi*].

David Atkinson, Belfast poet, has published nationally and internationally, and broadcast by the BBC. He has two collections, Thomas (2005) and Black-eyed Peace (2014), including the Pushcart nominated poem "Hunting for the Aurora". He was long-listed for the Seamus Heaney Award for New Writing 2017 @ablackeyedpeace www.davidatkinsonpoet.wordpress.com

Janet Barbaritz *Writing is a necessity, sharing it a privilege.* Janet Barbaritz, a Chapel Hillian originally from Buffalo, continues to appreciate the support and inspiration gained from writers in the Wednesdays at 1:00 poetry group. Janet's poems have appeared in the last two Heron Clan collections.

Maria Barrett, is a New Orleans writer, artist, and social advocate currently working on public education reform while pursuing a degree in Journalism.

Erin J. Bauman is a freelance writer who focuses on writing poetry that highlights social/environmental justice issues. Find Erin J. Bauman, The Panoptical Poet: online @ https://dharmaw.wixsite.com/mysite on Facebook @ https://www.facebook.com/erinjbaumanthepanopticalpoet/ on Twitter @ https://twitter.com/PanopticalPoet on YouTube @ https://www.youtube.com/channel/UCXjMbvu058wVc8eKNXBsfrw

Jacqueline Belle is a poet and voice artist. Jacqueline has two published poetry collections, *When I Walk Upon the Earth* and *The Collection: a poetic exploration of friendship, love, fantasies and the soulmate* (Honorable Mention in Reader's Favorite Book Award 2020). Watch for her upcoming poetry collection, *Synapses,* early 2021.

Trish Bennett grew up on the Rep. of Ireland/UK border. She spent her youth changing jobs, careers, and cities, not realising that she was building up a lifetime of shenanigans to tap into later on, when she gave in to the urge to write. **Website:** trishbennettwriter.com

Mitch Bensel is a multi-genre author, parent, and grandparent. He has written and produced spoken word CD's of poetry, healing, and guidance. Currently recording a new poetry CD and working on a murder mystery. His books can be intense but love always wins in the end.

Arlene S Bice is author of non-fiction books and recipient of the Florence Poets Society *Poet of Distinction Award*, published in several anthologies, and a member of TAF, IWWG, and WAM. Her column, *The Reading Corner*, appeared for ten years in the Register News. She lives in South Hill, Virginia.

Margaret Bockting writes poetry, draws pictures, and listens to her husband play guitar and to her son talk about pickleball at her home in Chapel Hill, NC. She enjoys walking her dogs and chatting with neighbors.

S. T. Brant is a teacher from Las Vegas. Pubs in/coming from EcoTheo, Door is a Jar, Santa Clara Review, Rain Taxi, New South, Green Mountains Review, Another Chicago Magazine, Ekstasis, 8 Poems, a few others. He's on Twitter @terriblebinth and Instagram @shanelemagne.

Paul Brookes has published seven books of poetry. His latest appeared in 2020 and is *Our Ghost's Holiday.* He is editor of The Wombwell Rainbow Interviews and lives in a cat house full of teddy bears. https://thewombwellrainbow.com

David Butler's poetry collections are Via Crucis (Doghouse, 2011) and All the Barbaric Glass (Doire, 2017), with a third collection, Liffey Sequence, forthcoming from Doire in 2021. His third published novel, City of Dis (New Island) was shortlisted for the Irish Novel of the Year, 2015.

Joan Canby has her MFA from Vermont College of Fine Arts. She spent her career as a technical writer. She's been published in: Frogpond, Main Street Rag, Broken Plate, and California Quarterly. Her upcoming book Cascades will be published by Assure Press. She is a native of Santa Barbara currently living in Dallas.

Nancy Corson Carter, Professor Emerita of Humanities at Eckerd College, has three poetry books—*Dragon Poems, The Sourdough Dream Kit,* and *A Green Bough: Poems for Renewal (2019)*—and three chapbooks. She's a gardener, swimmer, (in non Covid times) and environmentalist living in Chapel Hill, NC with her husband.

Glenn Cassidy teaches economics and public policy at the University at Albany at SUNY. His social science training often influences his creative writing. He has published poetry and short fiction in a number of anthologies and literary journals including M*ain Street Rag*, *Redheaded Stepchild*, *Prime Number Magazine*, and *Kakalak.*

Kristine Chalifoux is a poet and teacher who lives in Wake Forest; though not a North Carolina native, she's come to feel that the tar heel state is home. She is currently working on a manuscript, "Glass," she hopes to complete by the end of 2021.

Patty Cole writes poetry and essays. She lives in western Chatham County, NC, with her husband, Hoyt. Her first book of poetry A Way I Sing was published in 2015 by Main Street Rag Publishing. She garnered two distinctions from the North Carolina Poetry Society for her Poet Laureate Poem and the Katherine Kennedy Light Verse contests. She derives inspiration for writing from nature and music.

Linda M. Crate's works have been published in numerous magazines and anthologies both online and in print. She is the author of six chapbooks, including: *More Than Bone Music* (Clare Songbirds Publishing House, March 2019), and one novel *Phoenix Tears* (Czykmate Books, June 2018). Her full-length poetry collections are *Vampire Daughter* (Dark Gatekeeper Gaming, February 2020), *The Sweetest Blood* (Cyberwit, February 2020), and *Mythology of My Bones* (Cyberwit, August 2020).

Robert Cumming is a writer and teacher living in Durham. He's published poems in *The Southern Anthology: South Carolina* and elsewhere. With Montri Umavijani and Deborah Cumming, he edited and made translations for *A Premier Book of Contemporary Thai Verse.*

Bill Cushing : Raised in New York, Bill Cushing lived in numerous states, the Virgin Islands, and Puerto Rico after leaving the Navy and returning to college later in life. He moved to California after earning an MFA in writing from Goddard College and recently retired after teaching college English in Los Angeles.

Steve Cushman is the author of three novels and the poetry collection, *How Birds Fly.*

Stevie O. Daniels is the author of The Wild Lawn Handbook: Alternatives to the Traditional Front Lawn. Her poems have appeared in Heron Clan, Cairn, and the Marquis. An editor for FHI 360 in Durham, N.C., she is former assistant horticulturist for Juniper Level Botanic Garden. She holds degrees in English and horticulture.

David Dasher studied English Literature at UNC Greensboro and Loyola Chicago. He published a few poems when he was young and carefree, but then he didn't write poetry for ten years, and life was bleak. Five years ago, he started writing again. Yay! He lives in Chapel Hill, NC.

Dan J. Decker, besides writing poetry, is also an author of fiction and non-fiction books, an educator, lecturer, screenplay consultant, world traveler, dual citizen US/EU, formerly the Producing Artistic Director of the Las Vegas Shakespeare Company, and most of all, a grandfather. You can find him www.Amazon.com/author/dan.decker.

Diane Elayne Dees lives in Covington, Louisiana. Diane has published poetry, short fiction and creative nonfiction in numerous journal. She also publishes Women Who Serve, a blog covering women's professional tennis. Her chapbook*, I Can't Recall Exactly When I Died*, is forthcoming from Clare Songbirds Publishing House. Also forthcoming, from Kelsay Books, is Diane's chapbook, *Coronary Truth*. Diane's author blog is Diane Elayne Dees, Poet and Writer-at-Large.

Ginger Dehlinger is recognized primarily for her novels (*Brute Heart*, *Never Done*) Ginger Dehlinger's poetry has been published in numerous journals and anthologies, including Heron Clan. She also writes short stories and has won two Pacific Northwest writing competitions for her essays. You can find Ginger in Bend, Oregon or at www.gdehlinger.blogspot.com

Peach Delphine is a queer poet from Tampa, Florida. Infatuated with what remains of the undeveloped Gulf coast. This poem first appeared in Feral Poetry.

John C. Dendy: Raised in an Alabama coal mining camp, worked my way through college shoveling coal for 79¢/hour. Retired engineer, executive. Have lived in AZ, CA, NY, TX, Provence. Love the Mountain West, cooking, tennis, writing, singing, piano, my young-at-heart wife, an 84-year-old convertible, and Life. Honorable Mention, 2020 Reuben Rose competition.

Kitty Donnelly is a mental health services worker and award winning poet who is widely published, including as the joint winner of Indigo Dreams Collection Competition in 2019 for her book *The Impact of Limited Time."* She lives in West Yorkshire withhusband, daughter, terrier Zip and cat Pepper.

Frank Doonan, a Native farm boy from Rockville MD was born July 29, 1946. Resident of Hillsborough, NC for 13 years. BS in Agriculture Oklahoma State University 1970. Soil Scientist, Geologist, Paramedic, Carpenter, Plumber and whatever. Published in Heron Clan III and V. Founder Orange Dog Poet Society 2007, Performs Mime, standup comedy and Burlesque, and sometimes writes poetry.

Matt Duggan was born in Bristol 1971 and now lives in Newport, Wales with his partner Kelly. His poems have appeared in many journals including *Potomac Review, The Blue Nib, The High Window, Confluence, Marble and Polarity.* In nadition to many prizes, Matt has two chapbooks: *One Million Tiny Cuts* (Clare Song Birds Publishing House) and *A Season in Another World* (Thirty West Publishing House). His second full collection *Woodworm* (Hedgehog Poetry Press) was published in July 2019

Kapardeli Eftichi has a Doctorate from ARTS AND CULTURE WORLD ACADEMY. She lives in Patras, Greece. She writes poetry, stories, short stories, haiku, essays. She has studied journalism from A.K.E.M. and has many awards in national competitions. She has many national and international anthologies to her credit. She is a member of the World Poets' society.

Mary Elmahdy: Poetry is my teacher, my guide through old age, a way to reflect, examine, ponder, and often appear totally lazy to others, while finally enjoying the hell out of my life. Not able to call myself poet yet, but my thinking becomes continuously refined by the craft.

Patience Getrude Osime Emakele is a researcher and public affairs commentator who is passionate about changing the world through songs, poems and spoken words. Her passion for systemic and attitudinal change gave birth to Family and National Development Initiative where she points the torch light on family functionality as the foundation of a progressive nation.

Emmanuel O. Evans is a rational thinker, keen to expand skills and knowledge, a writer, lover of art, teachable, self-motivated and result-oriented. A customer relationship management expert, service-oriented, loves data and data analysis. A proud Pisces who loves nature, humanity and God."

Attracta Fahy's background is in Nursing/Social Care. She lives in Co.Galway, Ireland, works as a Psychotherapist, and is mother to three children. She earned her MA in Writing NUIG in 2017. She was nominated for Pushcart 2018, and Best of the Web 2019, Her first collection was published by Fly on the Wall in March 2020.

Kari Flickinger is the author of 'The Gull and the Bell Tower' (Femme Salvé Books, December 2020). Her work has been nominated for Best of the Net and the SFPA Rhysling Award. She is an alumna of UC Berkeley and the Community of Writers.

Emilie Fox lives in Northern California with her family. She enjoys long walks with her dog, as well as experimenting with writing poetry and other forms of creative expression. Her work has been published in local literary anthologies Impressions (2015), Havik: Magic Tricks (2019) and Homeward (2020).

Mary Kay Fruga is a Wisconsin native now living in Raleigh, N.C., where she retired from an unlikely career that combined teaching, human resources and IT. She enjoys gardening, cooking and playing with words. Mary Kay is currently working on her first chap book and exploring opportunities for publication.

Dai Fry is a poet living on the south coast of England. Originally from Swansea. Wales was and still is a huge influence on his work.
Twitter: @thnargg Web: seekingthedarklight.co.uk
Published by: Black Bough Poetry, Re-Side, The Hellebore Press, Pangolin Review, Morepork Press.and The Failure Baler.

Michael Gaspeny is the author of *The Tyranny of Questions*, a novella in verse, and the chapbooks *Re-Write Men* and *Vocation.* Winner of the Randall Jarrell Poetry Prize and the O. Henry Festival Story Competition, he has received The NC Governor's Award for Volunteer Excellence for his hospice service.

As a rock journalist, **Randy Gerritse** watches the world in search of both rhythms and answers. As an author, known Twitter poet, and lyricist, poetry is part of his every day and even found its way into his novels. His first self-publication "The Rhythm of Life" is available on Amazon.

Jonathan Giles, a self-employed writer, hosts weekly virtual workshops in poetry and narrative writing. His poems have appeared in *Main Street Rag*, *Avalon*, *Dead Mule,* and *Delta Poetry Review*, among others. In 2020 he was a finalist in the Applewhite Poetry Award sponsored by the *North Carolina Literary Review.*

Catherine Graham is an award-winning poet, novelist and creative-writing instructor. Her sixth poetry collection, *The Celery Forest,* was named a CBC Best Book of the Year. Publications include *Poetry Daily, Arc Poetry Magazine, Glasgow Review of Books, Joyland, Poetry Ireland, Gutter, The Malahat Review. Æther: an out-of-body lyric* is forthcoming as is her second novel, *The Most Cunning Heart,* www.catherinegraham.com @catgrahampoet

Sinead Griffin's poetry has been published in *Channel Magazine, Skylight 47* and *The Irish Times Hennessy New Irish Writing.* She placed second in the *Reclaim the Vision of 1916* Poetry Prize, was shortlisted for the FISH Poetry Prize 2020. She lives in Dublin with her husband and three daughters.
Susan Grimshaw is a retired graphic designer living in San Francisco. She has a published collection of poetry from 1993: Black Hat, Blue Veil, Starry Sky; and is writing again after a long hiatus, since a chance meeting on Twitter with an outstanding poet.

Chitisha Gunno holds a degree in Applied IT, but also with an early rich literary background: Shakespeare, Salman Rushdie, Jane Austen, Virginia Wolf, thus this love for writing. She hails from Mauritius, works at the local Ministry of Education, and is part of YALI movement. Her blog is living136.wordpress.com,

Kari Gunter-Seymour's poetry collections include *A Place So Deep Inside America It Can't Be Seen* (Sheila-Na-Gig Editions 2020) and *Serving* (Crisis Chronicles Press 2020). Her poems appear in numerous journals and publications including *Verse Daily, Rattle, The NY Times* and on her website: www.karigunterseymourpoet.com. She is the 2020 Ohio Poet of the Year and Poet Laureate of Ohio.

Aruna Gurumurthy is an Indian American poet with seven full length volumes who writes about life's journey toward peace, and philosophical subjects that cover a diversity of human experience.Her recent work is in sestina form.

John Guzlowski's poems and stories have appeared in such national journals as North American Review, Ontario Review, Rattle, Atlanta Review, Nimrod, Crab Orchard Review, and Salon.com. His book *Echoes of Tattered Tongues* about his parents' lives during and after the Holocaust won the Eric Hoffer/Montaigne Award for most thought provoking book of 2017. His mystery novels have been reviewed by the New York Times.

Dorna Hainds lives in a small town in Michigan. Her introduction to Haiku came shortly after back surgery in the early 2000s. She has been reading/writing Haiku for nearly a decade now. Most of her Haiku inspirations are found in her daily life.

Nicola Harrison: Professional singer, author, scriptwriter and educator Nicola has written 3 books about poetry and music, three music poems and published 2 poetry pamphlets. A performance poet, she is also lecturer in song and interpretation at Pembroke College Oxford U.K.

Ho Haryadi, organizational consultant and retired psychiatrist, moved here from Western New York with his late wife in 2007, now lives in Hillsborough, NC with his two boy cats. Shares life's multifaceted notions and experiences through the lens of poetry found at Wednesdays@One since joining in 2019.

These poems are from **Lola Haskins'** most recent collection: *Asylum, Improvisations on John Clare* (U Pittsburgh Press, 2019), whose highly varied sections –including a humor one--parallel Clare's journey when he escaped one of the insane asylums in which he lived most of his adult life. Visit her at lolahaskins.com

Nadine Hayes' debut poetry book "Paper Hearts" is available on Amazon. This is her first year as an editor for the Heron Clan. Aside from reading and writing, Nadine loves walking with her dog Faith and is pursuing a career in forensic psychology .(Editor, HC VIII)

Kelly A. Hegi is a writer currently living in Minneapolis, Minnesota with her husband, three kids and two dogs. She is a licensed minister, an active Spiritual Director and writes to explore everyday life from a more creative lens. She has just begun to get published and is still stunned every time it happens.

Thomas Hines is Professor Emeritus of Comparative Literature at Kent State University. He moved to North Carolina in 2007 and lives with his wife, Susan, and their dog and horses in Fuquay-Varina. He has published five books of poetry, each in collaboration with a painter.

Wendy Holborow's, poetry has been published internationally and placed in competitions. She gained a Master's in Creative Writing at Swansea University, Wales. Recent collections include: *An Italian Afternoon* (Indigo Dreams 2017) a Poetry Book Society Pamphlet Choice, *Janky Tuk Tuks* (The High Window Press 2018) and *Shipwrecked*, (2020). More information on: www.wendyholborow.org.uk

Ho Haryadi is an organizational consultant and retired psychiatrist who moved here from Western New York with his late wife in 2007, now lives in Hillsborough, NC with his two boy cats and shares life's multifaceted notions and experiences through the lens of poetry found at Wednesdays@One since joining in 2019.

Earl Carlton Huband is the author of *The Innocence of Education* [Longleaf Press, 2018] and *In the Coral Reef of the Market* [Main Street Rag Publishing, 2020]. Both chapbooks are based on Huband's experiences many years ago as a Peace Corps Volunteer in the Sultanate of Oman.

Olaitan Humble is a writer of African heritage. He is an aviphile and pacifist who enjoys reading satire, and collecting quotations and astrophotos. A Pushcart Prize nominee, his work appears in CP Quarterly, The African Writers Review, Arts Lounge, Luna Luna Magazine, Rigorous, Nymphs, AGNG, NINSHAR Arts, and Doubleback Review, among others. IG/Twitter: @olaitanhumble.

Linda Imbler is the author of five paperback poetry collections and three e-book collections (Soma Publishing.) This writer lives in Wichita, Kansas with her husband, Mike the Luthier, several quite intelligent saltwater fish, and an ever-growing family of gorgeous guitars. Learn more at lindaspoetryblog.blogspot.com.

S. L. Jaerin, also known as "Sye", is an artist and a writer currently living in Nebraska. He enjoys using both digital and traditional media in art, as well as writing both poetry and prose, preferring fantasy and character poems.

Mary Jaimes-Serrano is an author of romance novels and poetry. She has a BA in Law and Society from Penn State University and is preparing to study her MFA next fall. She Edits the Heron Clan. She can be found on Twitter @MaryJaimesSerr1 or on her website dedicated to her books and poetry @ mjaimesserrano.com. .(Editor, HC VIII)

Debbie Johnson is a poet, singer, watercolorist and fabric artist living in Raleigh, NC. She writes of love, fanciful fictional people, and her experiences growing up as an army brat. Look for her poetry collection at postpoems.org/authors/djtj. Her blog and art can be found at djtjohnson.com.

Jerry Judge is the author of seven poetry chapbooks. He lives in Cincinnati where he facilitates the poetry group for Cincinnati Writers Project. A Pushcart nominee, his work has been published in numerous journals and anthologies. He spends many hours volunteering at no-kill animal shelters.

Gaynor Kane lives in Belfast Northern Ireland. She has three poetry collections, and is co-author of a fourth all published by Hedgehog Poetry Press. In 2019, she won the Seventh Annual Bangor Poetry Competition. Find out more about Gaynor at her website: www.gaynorkane.com.

Christine Kelly, an emerging writer living in Illinois, can be found scribbling poems on scraps of paper, often while in church. Her work has previously been published in *The Wood Knots, A Poetry Collection*, *Voice of Eve*, *Heron Clan VII* and *Medium* magazine's *PS I Love You* and *Loose Words.*

Margaret Koger is a Lascaux Prize finalist and school media specialist with a writing habit. She lives near the river in Boise, Idaho and writes to give voice to all earthlings. See more poems at: Amsterdam Quarterly, Thimble, Trouvaille Review, Tiny Seed Literary Journal, Ponder Savant, Subjectiv, and Last Leaf.

Renata Lader's talents include writing, pine-needle basketry, photography, painting, jewelry-making, Faberge and Ukrainian egg-making, quilling and quilting. She has published poems in Contemporary American Voices, Heron Clan Anthology, The Final Draft, The Sounds of Poets Cooking anthology, and The Village Rambler. She published "You People, a Memoir of an Immigrant House-Cleaning Lady." Forthcoming is a memoir about experiences during Communism and the Solidarity workers' movement in Poland. She lives in Raleigh, NC. www.RenataUniqueGifts.etsy.com

D.L. Lang is the author of 13 poetry books, most recently This Festival of Dreams. She served as poet laureate of Vallejo, California from 2017 to 2019. Her poems have been transformed into songs, Jewish liturgy, and used to advocate for peace and justice. Find her at poetryebook.com

June Logue is a graduate of Douglas College. She studied poetry with John Ciardi at Rutgers and with Mary Jo Bang at the New School. She was a Special Education teacher in New Jersey for twenty years. She has been a member of Wednesdays@One poetry group in Chapel Hill for two years. Her work appeared in *Heron Clan VI.*

Kolawole Oluwabukola Lovelin is an experienced African poet, Movie director and upcoming linguist. She tapped her life story when writing her first poem "DREAMS." She is a fresh soul in a young Nigerian body whose poetry seeks to delve and awaken human consciousness. Her first series of poems includes: Agony of an African Man, Choice and Black is Beautiful.

Lennart Lundh is a poet, short-fictionist, historian, and photographer. His work has appeared internationally since 1965. Len may be contacted at LenLundh@aol.com.

Ed Lyons has lived and written poetry in PA, FL, VA and NC. One of three founders of the Heron Clan, (with Doug Stuber and Richard Smyth) his latest Chapbook is "Wachovia" a history of the Moravian church in verse. Order books directly at edlyons2929@gmail.com. He writes Hymns for Trinity Moravian, Winston-Salem, NC

Charlotte Mandel's eleventh book of poetry is titled *Alive and In Use: Poems in the Japanese Form of Haibun* (Kelsay Books). Her awards include: Lifetime Achievement Award from Brooklyn College; New Jersey Poets Prize; two fellowships in poetry from New Jersey State Council on the Arts. Visit her at charlottemandel.com.

Todd Irwin Marshall - Ph.D. in Luso-Brazilian Literature, UNC-Chapel Hill. Currently lives and works in Belo Horizonte, Brazil, where he is an English teacher, translator, and poet. Published a bilingual book of poetry entitled "Canções Urbanas Vi Tais / Urban Song Vi Tals"; his poetry has also been published in a number of anthologies in both the USA and Brazil.

Tim Mattimoe lives in Pittsboro with his wife Karen, near their three children and four grandchildren. He writes poems that honor the past, both his own and others. He s a member of the Friday Noon Poets in Chapel Hill.

Michael Maul is a 2019 "Best of the Net" poetry nominee, and the author of the poetry collection Dancing Naked in Front of Dogs (2018). In 2019 he issued a chapbook, Birds Who Eat French Fries. Maul is the winner of the Mercantile Library Prize for Fiction and was twice
longlisted for the International Fish Poetry Prize.

Anne McMaster is from Northern Ireland. Living on an old farm near the rural north coast, her work focuses on small moments of quiet beauty and her observations of the natural world.Her poetry has been published in the UK, in Ireland and the USA. Her first collection of poetry was published in May 2020 by Hedgehog Press.

Deborah Melone lives and writes poetry in Watertown, MA. She teaches ESL to adult learners from many countries in the Watertown Library. Her published books are Farmers' Market and The Wheel of the Year. She enjoys writing about food, scientific subjects, art, family and friends.

Michael Menut, of NC, contributes these poems as a reflection of the darkness that we've persisted through in 2020. His writing carries a depth that eerily plunges through topics as diverse as philosophy, politics, musical inspiration and the turn of the seasons. Hiking and photography keep his creative spirit thriving.

Nastashia Minto is the author of Naked: The Rhythm and Groove of It. The Depth and Length to It. An African American woman born in South Georgia. Her life experiences led her to obtain an associate degree in occupational therapy, a bachelor's degree in psychology and she is currently working on a PhD in Depth Psychology.

Phodiso Modirwa is a Motswana writer and poet with works published on The Kalahari Review, Ake Review, Jalada Africa, The Weight Of Years: An Afroanthology of Creative Nonfiction, Praxis Online Magazine and elsewhere. She is a recipient of the Botswana President's Award-Contemporary Poetry 2016.

Karen Mooney's poetry has been published in USA, UK and Ireland. Her co- written pamphlet with Gaynor Kane, *Penned In*, was published recently by The Hedgehog Poetry Press and she is excited to be working towards one of her own in 2021.

Bennett Myers is an eighty-seven year old North Carolina native who has been a poet only since 1991 when he was led into writing by Rumi translator Coleman Barks. He writes about things in the world that say, write me. These poems are often drawn from deep and emotional places, even taking on old age and death and some humor creeps in.

Toti O'Brien is the Italian Accordionist with the Irish Last Name. Born in Rome, living in Los Angeles, she is an artist, musician and dancer. She is also the author of *Other Maidens* (BlazeVOX, 2020), *An Alphabet of Birds* (Moonrise, 2020) and *Pages of a Broken Diary* (Pski's Porch 2021).

Kenton Oliver is a poet and dreamer from Canada who strives to share inspiring words straight from the heart. He appreciates philosophy, psychology, music, rhythm, and beautiful words. Check out Kenton's website - ataraxy.ca - to find all his poetry and social media links.

Jakky Bankong-Obi writes from Abuja, Nigeria. She is Co-Editor at Icefloe Press. Her work has been featured/forthcoming in London Grip, The Kalahari Review, Amberflorazine, Zarf Poetry, Gutter Magazine, Hobartpulp, Pidgeonholes, Reliquiae Journal (Corbel Stone Press), Memento; An Anthology of Contemporary Nigerian Poetry and others. She enjoys long walks, yoga & dabbling in nature photography. Jakky is on Twitter as @jakkybee

Andy Oram is a writer and editor at O'Reilly Media, a highly respected book publisher and technology information provider. Print publications include The Economist, The Journal of Information Technology & Politics, and Vanguardia Dossier. He has published in Arlington Literary Journal, Offcourse and Panapoly.

Lucía Orellana-Damacela is the author of the poetry collections *Inherent* (2020), *Longevity River* (2019), *Sea of Rocks* and *Life Lines* (2018). Her work has been published in English and Spanish in venues such as *PANK, Tin House Online, Carve, Frontera* and more. She tweets at @lucyda and blogs at notesfromlucia.wordpress.com.

Stephen Page is part Native American. He was born in Detroit. He holds degrees from Palomar College, Columbia University, and Bennington College. He loves his wife, family, friends, spontaneous road trips, long walks through woodlands, environmental protection, rainstorms, stomping on his cell phone, and making noise with his electric bass.

Bernard Perason: his work has appeared in many publications, including *Aesthetica Magazine, Four by Four, The Gentian, The Poetry Village Crossways* a selection of his poetry 'In Free Fall' was published by *Leaf by Leaf Press*. In 2019 he won second prize in The Aurora Prize (An international Competition in Poetry) for "Manor Farm."

Marc Puricelli is a professional pianist and composer re-located from New York where he performed, recorded and toured with many luminaries. His first poem was published when he was in the eighth. grade and he has continued to explore his love of words, lyrics and poetry.

Khalisa Rae is a poet and journalist in Durham, NC, and author of Real Girls Have Real Problems chapbook. Her poetry can be seen in *Crab Fat, Damaged Goods, Hellebore, Terse, Sundog Lit, PANK Tishman Review, the Obsidian,* among others. She is the winner of the Bright Wings Poetry contest, the Furious Flower Gwendolyn Brooks Poetry Prize, the White Stag Publishing Contest, among others. Currently, she serves as Managing Equity Editor at Carve Magazine and Writing Center Director at Shaw University. Her debut collections, *Ghost in a Black Girls Throat* are forthcoming from Red Hen Press in 2021.

November Rhodes is a poet, novelist, and painter based in Minnesota. Art helps her take the mess in her brain and turn it into beautiful creations. November has had poems published in one prior literary journal and has a poetry and art book, "Afterglow," published on Amazon.

Carolyn Robinson is a talented writer who leaves it all on the page every time she pens a poem. She is a talented writer, an actress as well as a performing arts instructor. She enjoys being the grandmother to five and resides in Baltimore, MD.

LaVan Robinson is a writer from Philadelphia, now living in Lancaster, PA. He is a 13 year military veteran. He has 3 books of poetry books on Amazon and Kindle. He has a 35 year old son named Audy. He loves poetry because poetry chose him.

Delia Ross writes under the pen name POEETERNAL. Her ad-free blog is www.poeeternal.com. Stop by and tell her which ones you like.

Louise Runyon: A dancer/choreographer as well as poet, Louise is Artistic Director of Louise Runyon Performance Company and has toured the nation with her one-woman show. Based in Western NC, she has published four books of poetry and is a lifelong activist. www.LouiseRunyonPerformance.com

Folasade Scott is a 40-year-old native of California, living in Winston-Salem since 2012. She received a Master of Arts in Teaching - Special Education from Winston-Salem State University and a degree in American Studies with an emphasis in Social Psychology, the Arts and Education from the University of California Berkeley. She enjoys utilizing visual art and poetry to educate, encourage, guide, awaken, inspire

Sanjeev Sethi is published in over thirty countries. His poems are in more than 350 journals or online literary venues. *Wrappings in Bespoke* is joint-winner of Full Fat Collection Competition-Deux organized by the Hedgehog Poetry Press UK. It's his fourth full-length collection and latest release. He lives in Mumbai, India.

Paul Sherman reads and writes poetry from the portion of Mt. Mitchell that's in Yancey County, North Carolina. Some of his work can be found in the anthologies of Old Mountain Press. He works at Wildacres, an artist retreat on the Blue Ridge Parkway in Little Switzerland, NC.

Sybil Austin Skakle has two books of poetry *Searchings: Rocks Revelations, Rainbows* (2002) and *Loves and Lives of Living and Loving* (2002). She has three memoires including *"Confessions of an Outer Banks Filly"* (2009). She compiled and edited *The Story of the Amity United Methodist Church* and a young adult novel *Who Plays on Court One* (2018).

Angelaurelio Soldi is a retired Physics Professor living with his wife Jerry in an old farmhouse in Orange County near Hillsborough, NC. He has published (Lulu,com) ten books of poetry, a translation of Dante's Inferno and two books of painting with poems by Tom Hines.

Shelby Stephenson was poet laureate of North Carolina 2015-2018. His most recent book is *Slavery and Freedom on Paul's Hill.* Among many other honors, his 2008 book *Family: Homage to July, the Slave Girl* won the Bellday Prize in 2008.

Cindy B. Stevens lives in Hillsborough, NC. She posts poem snippets every six days: justplaineclectic.blogspot.com, Facebook; @cindybstevenspoet Her poetry appears in Pfeiffer University's literary journal, The Phoenix; and Heron Clan anthologies. She enjoys live audiences, so after quarantine, will return to open mics. Main Street Rag published her chapbook, *Naked.*

Julie Stevens writes poems that sometimes reflect the impact Multiple Sclerosis has on her life. Her poems have recently been published on The Blue Nib, Dodging the Rain, Ariel Chart and The Honest Ulsterman. Her debut chapbook, *Quicksand,* was published by Dreich in September 2020. Her website is www.jumpingjulespoetry.com.

Michelle G. Stradford uses empowering self-love prose and affirmations to uplift others as they navigate life's challenges. Tackling serious issues, her poetry encourages all to strengthen their resolve to overcome setbacks and trauma to emerge more resilient. Michelle's writes contemporary free verse that is relatable and connects with her readers.

Samuel Strathman is a poet, author, educator, and editor at Cypress: A Poetry Journal. His debut chapbook, "In Flocks of Three to Five" was published by Anstruther Press. His second chapbook, "The Incubus" will be in print this fall (Roaring Junior Press, 2020).

Jake Street is a poet from London and student at Lancaster University. He has been published in Paper Swans Press' Anthology of Young Poets and in the 2018 Tower Poets anthology Hatch a Blue Sky. He runs Lancaster's Poetry Cafe open mic events.

Caren Stuart is an award-winning poet/writer/artist/maker living in Chatham County, NC with husband and cat. She's a longtime NC Poetry Society member, habitual volunteer for arts organizations, sole proprietor/creator of "convoluted notions" one of a kind art and craft, and
frequent attendee/organizer of all manner of artsy/writerly events.

Doug Stuber is a poet, artist, musician, professor, journalist who, with Ed Lyons and Richard Smyth founded the Heron Clan in 1996. Twelve volumes of poetry and an array of publications pale in comparison to the joy derived from being friends with so many poets.

Dr Priya Dolma Tamang. I am a medical graduate, tribal Nepali by origin and Indian by nationality. Though English is not my native language, I write poetry in English for the sheer relief and joy it brings me.

Kamil Tangalychev is Poet Laureate of Mordovia. The award-winning Russian journalist, essayist, and poet has produced eight books of poetry. He was anthologized in *Poetry of the Third Millennium* (Moscow). An ethnic Tatar, Tangalychev has been translated from Russian into several minority languages of Russians: Moksha, Erzya, and Tatar. Translator Bio:

Dean Furbish lives in Raleigh, NC. Nominated for a Pushcart Prize, his literary translations have appeared in *Chiron Review, Euphony Journal, International Poetry Review, Metamorphoses, North Dakota Quarterly, Poetry East, Poetry Salzburg Review, Ponder Review, Quarterly West, Two Thirds North, Xavier Review*, and elsewhere.

Annette (Wengert) Tarpley (USA) has won numerous awards/accolades, has many poems published online, playlist of recitations on YouTube, and is published through anthologies. Annette's first book: Poetry Potpourri; co-authored, "Uplifting"; and "Two Heart's, with Sarfraz Ahmed to release spring 2021. Founder/administrator: The Passion of Poetry, an administrator for "Motivational Strips," Facebook sites.

Aurélien Thomas is a poet who lives in London (England). 'A Thought' is part of 'A Vow', his first poetry collection in English. You can follow him on his writing blog (aurelienthomas.org) and/ or Burning Words Poetry (his Youtube channel).

Lisa Tomey is a poet and writer from Raleigh, NC. Publications include: Heart Sounds chapbook, two anthologies, and several literary publications. Tomey is currently working on an anthology, Heart Beats. An editor of poetry, she is on the editorial team for Fine Lines Literary Journal.

Phil Venable's record label Soul City Sounds recently released the debut poetry album by NC Poet Laureate Jaki Shelton Green. This poem marks his return to writing after many years pursuing a career in music. He lives in Chapel Hill with his partner, the poet Shannon Jackson, and his children, Jett and Dash.

Tuur Verheyde is a twenty-three year old Belgian poet. Tuur writes poetry exclusively in English, even though Dutch is his first language. His work often discusses current events, progressive politics, spirituality, highbrow and popular culture as well as personal experiences and stories.

Patricia Walsh of Burnfort, Co Cork, was educated at University College Cork, (MA in Archaeology). Her poetry has been published in Stony Thursday; Southword; Narrator International, and many others. A chapbook, titled Continuity Errors in 2010, and a novel, The Quest for Lost Éire, in 2014."Outstanding Balance," is scheduled for publication in 2021. She was the featured poet in the inaugural edition of Fishbowl Magazine, and is a regular at the O Bheal poetry night in Cork city.

Mali Warshofsky Born in Poland. Lived in Israel until the age of 18. Moved to Monroe, NY with her husband. She has two sons. Moved to Chapel Hill NC six years ago. English is her 4th acquired language after Polish, Hebrew, and Yiddish. She is studying Spanish. She chooses to write in English.

Delaney Watson was a sharp-eyed editor of the Heron Clan, accountant, mystic, philosopher and generous friend. A volume of his selected work will appear posthumously.

Jennifer Joyce Webber enjoys reading, writing, playing music, gardening, cooking, and hiking when not working as a school psychologist. During quarantine she is enjoying having more time for writing and being with family. She previously published one poem. She lives with her husband, daughters, and dog in North Carolina.

Priscilla Webster-Williams lives to write poetry in Durham, North Carolina. She has been known to experiment with a form called Ambling Sonics; an example is in this anthology: "Poem after Ferlinghetti's Be a Poet or a Researcher." Her chapbook of poems, *The Narrative Possibilities of Coral,* was published by Main Street Rag.

Michael J. Whelan is an Irish soldier-poet and historian. He served as a UN peacekeeper in Lebanon and Kosovo. His poetry collections Peacekeeper (2016) and Rules of Engagement (2019) are published by Doire Press. He holds an MA in Modern History from the National University of Ireland Maynooth.

Kristie L. Williams – received a B.A. in English/Creative Writing from Saint Andrews Presbyterian College and a MA Ed. in Adult Education at East Carolina University. Published by Main Street Rag, Dan River Review, Cairn, Maximum Tilt Solstice Anthology, Madness Muse Press, Hermit Feathers Review and Voice Lux Journal. She advocates for people with disabilities via adaptive recreation, reading great books, and going to rock concerts.

Chanah Wizenberg received her BA from Hunter College in English and Creative Writing. Her poetry has appeared in several magazines. Chanah has been a professional ballerina, a pastry chef, and English teacher. She resides in Raleigh, North Carolina with her dog, Asha, and her cat, Marmalade.

Jocelyn Wright serves as Associate Professor in the Department of English Language and Literature at Mokpo National University in rural South Korea. jocelynmnu@yahoo.com

Sarah Wyman writes and teaches in the Hudson Valley. Her poetry has appeared in *Aaduna, Mudfish, Ekphrasis, San Pedro River Review, Potomac Review, Petrichor Review, Heron Clan VII*, *Chronogram*, and other venues. Her collection, *Fried Goldfinch*, is forthcoming at Codhill Press. Website: https://faculty.newpaltz.edu/sarahwyman/